Meals
In
Moments

Meals In Moments

by

Maggie Brogan

CONTENTS

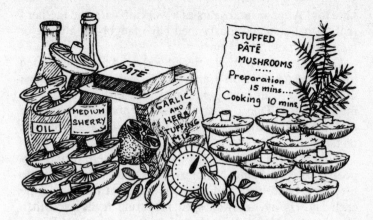

1 INTRODUCTION

More than ever before men and women are having to juggle the demands of work and home. Whether they are wives and mothers, divorcees bringing up children single-handed, lone fathers, people living alone or working couples, thousands are forced to limit their culinary skills to a frantic 30 or so minutes each evening.

Statistically, women still do the most cooking, with men more likely to eat out, buy ready-made meals or rely on the local pizza delivery service. But the high costs of these foods and the reduced income many are facing have led to a marked rise in the number of people rustling up an interesting meal, either for themselves and friends or for their families. These recipes are designed to be high on taste and low on hassle for those whose lives are too short to spend much time in the kitchen, yet without costing the earth.

As a home economist I have always been amused, and perhaps a little intrigued, at the way some men cook. Most love to experiment, throwing together a dollop of this and a handful of that in the hope that they produce a creative masterpiece. Which they usually do – and in whistle-stop time too! After several years as a working wife and mother I realise that subconsciously men have taught me a thing or two about cooking in a hurry.

Cooking is not a strict science and need not be confined to a straitjacket of do's and don'ts and musts and must nots. Allow your own personality and instinct to intrude into a recipe. Don't worry too much about weighing or measuring ingredients; rely instead, as all good cooks do, on taste.

Surveys have revealed that the whole pattern of the way people eat is changing. No longer does traditional family life revolve around meat and two veg served at the same time each day. The average time spent preparing meals is less than 10 minutes and members of the family often eat at different times. Lap meals in front of the television have become perfectly acceptable and convenience food is no longer the mark of a lazy individual.

Research also shows that many women actually prefer to spend their time working, pursuing hobbies and doing things with family and friends rather than trudging the eternal triangle of cooker, sink and dining table, and family life is benefiting, say the experts.

After a long tiring day, thinking of what to cook often presents the biggest problem. Sometimes we want to eat something which is nice and tasty but a bit different from a grilled chop and boiled vegetables. The last thing we want to do is spend precious time searching for a recipe which doesn't demand hours of slogging. All too often we end up reaching for the sausages or beefburgers and dragging out the chip pan.

Yet fast need not mean junk. By all means be choosy about convenience foods but don't feel guilty about using those which you can make work for you. Match the best of the manufactured with the choicest fresh ingredients.

Jam, bread, canned soup and even butter, are convenience foods yet they have been around so long we don't view them as such. Ready-made products like pasta, canned beans and vegetables are just a few convenience foods which are ideal in helping to prepare a quick meal.

But don't be fooled by them all. Some commercially prepared dishes can be much more expensive to buy than they would cost to make from scratch, and with very little saving in time and effort on your part.

How do you define quick and simple? Views may differ. My idea is to avoid recipes which demand too much fiddly preparation, although inevitably there must be some. And I hate having to use too many utensils, saucepans and dishes. Trying to re-create the banqueting department of the Savoy Hotel is not my idea of a stress-free evening!

This book aims to use as few ingredients as possible, and eliminate too much weighing and measuring. To cut down time spent shopping, most – if not all – of the ingredients are available from larger supermarkets. Yet it is a good idea for those constrained by budget to shop around for the cheapest price.

Most of the recipes featured can be prepared and cooked within 30 to 40 minutes, and in some cases even less. Also included are a few which are simple to prepare but take longer to cook. Sometimes, once a load of ingredients has been thrown into a pot, it's nice to relax with a glass of wine while a meal bubbles away in the oven.

The dishes can also be as simple or exotic as you choose. For instance, you can make a quick and cheap sauce for pasta by frying a sliced onion and some crushed garlic in a little oil, adding a can of chopped tomatoes, a few bruised leaves of oregano and a dash or two of Tabasco sauce then topping with a generous dusting of Parmesan cheese. The result? A family meal for less than the price of this book!

Depending on budget, the same sauce can be made more exotic with the addition of thinly sliced peppered salami, a few black olives, a handful of button mushrooms and a splash of red wine. In no time you can serve a meal fit for the most discerning connoisseur!

This book aims not just to give recipes but to stimulate the imagination and encourage improvisation. A book to dip into perhaps – an ideas book.

When you think about it, all recipes are just a variation on a theme. It is the way in which ingredients are combined, the

9

contrast in textures and blending of flavours and colours, which give each dish its own unique taste and appearance.

Experiment and have fun. Use the recipes as a basic guide, adding or substituting favourite ingredients until you create a dish to your own personal satisfaction.

2   WHAT'S IN STORE?

Dashing to the shops a few minutes before closing time for the odd item missing from a recipe does nothing to relieve the stress of after work cooking. A frantic ten minutes in the lunch hour, or a three mile drive to the late-night grocer isn't much good either. And neither is good if you are trying to live on a tight budget!

In an ideal world we would sit down for half an hour on a Sunday evening, plan our menus for the week and shop once for all the goods. But for most of us life just isn't that organised.

Concocting a meal becomes infinitely quicker if a range of versatile and non-perishable ingredients are to hand. A well-stocked store cupboard alleviates the stress of cooking when you are too tired, get in late or haven't had time to shop.

Often on such evenings impromptu guests arrive and, having boldly made the suggestion that they stay for supper, panic-stricken you try to visualise what lies lurking in the fridge/cupboard/larder. If you're anything like me it won't be much: a bit of mouldy cheese, half a can of fruit cocktail and a jar of mincemeat your mother made years ago! It won't do your reputation as a cook much good and you end up suggesting a take-away.

Vow to change things now! Actually, in order to write this book I have been forced to follow my own instructions and have been amazed how much easier and quicker cooking can be. Keeping at least some of the items listed in this chapter, tucked away in a cupboard, really does save time, energy and hassle.

Time spent shopping is drastically reduced because you only have to shop for fresh produce. Non-perishables can be replaced gradually which spreads the cost. Contrary to popular belief it is possible to eat nothing but dried, canned and frozen food and remain in perfect health.

Grains, pasta and pulses, which have a shelf life of six to 12 months, offer unlimited scope for knocking up quick and tasty meals. Often the simplest is the nicest. Try tossing a chunk of butter and some finely chopped garlic through freshly cooked tagliatelle and sprinkle liberally with Parmesan cheese.

Canned vegetables, fish and meat last in good condition for about one year provided they are stored correctly, i.e. in a cool, dry cupboard. Experiment with different combinations and various dressings, to make interesting salads.

Try a mixture of chick peas, red-brown beans, sliced artichoke hearts and sweet red peppers. Toss through a couple of tablespoons of Dark And Spicy Dressing (see page 84). For added substance and flavour, crumble over some feta cheese (which has a fridge-life of two months) or flaked tuna fish and a few black olives. Keep a packet of melba toast in the cupboard to serve with this type of salad.

Beans, lentils and rice can also be thrown together with a variety of herbs, spices and fresh vegetables to make tasty meals. (See chapter 8 on Pasta, Grains and Pulses.)

Cans of tomatoes are indispensable to the cook in a hurry. Several varieties are now available, including those with onion and chilli. Chopped tomatoes are useful for making all manner of sauce bases for meat, fish, pasta and vegetables. Even a simple sauce can lift an otherwise plain dish into something really brilliant.

It is worth keeping a few sun-dried tomatoes in stock.

These are fairly expensive and not that easy to find but because of their strong taste a few go a long way. Use them in salads as a stand-by, or smeared on pitta bread as a base for pizza-type toppings.

Stuffing mixes make ideal crunchy toppings and add taste and bulk to fish and vegetable dishes. With none of the chore of making breadcrumbs, varieties include apple, herb and garlic and herb and apricot as well as the traditional favourites.

Try brushing some lamb cutlets with beaten egg and then drop them one by one into a small polythene bag filled with parsley and thyme stuffing mix. Give the bag a shake and then simply remove the chops and cook them under the grill.

Indian naan bread is another good stand-by. Although the dough needs proving for an hour, so little work is involved. You simply roll it out and pop under the grill. The result is a deliciously scorched and puffy outside and a soft moist inside. Naan bread makes a good accompaniment to pulse and vegetable casseroles, stir-fries and kebabs. One packet will serve four people.

Although it's a useful stand-by to keep a few jars of dried herbs in the cupboard, nothing gives life to food more than the flavour of fresh herbs. Supermarkets don't always have a big selection in stock, which is frustrating especially if you have gone there in search of a particular variety.

Herbs are easy to grow and it saves time to keep a pot by the kitchen door. A basic supply includes parsley, chives, sage, thyme, chervil, mint, rosemary, basil and marjoram. All but mint and rosemary can be grown in a multi-planter (a big pot with holes in the side). Mint has invasive roots and should be planted in its own container, and rosemary grows into a bush and therefore needs more space.

Fresh herbs give a welcome 'bite' to dull salads. Try a mix of shredded iceberg lettuce and roughly chopped parsley, mint, chervil, tarragon and coriander. Toss in a well flavoured vinaigrette dressing – delicious!

There is no need to spend time and energy chopping fresh herbs to death. Take a few sprigs and chop just enough to bruise the leaves, thus releasing their aromatic flavour. Toss into dishes at the last minute.

13

Dried fruit has a shelf life of about three months and canned fruit about one year. Soak a selection overnight – apricots, apples, peaches – and then stew in a little water and demerara sugar until tender. Allow to cool and mix with some of the more exotic canned varieties – lychees, black cherries, melon – and serve with a scoop of good quality ice cream and one or two Continental-style biscuits.

A can of sweetened chestnut purée provides nature's instant dessert – purer and nicer than packets of 'chemical cocktail'. Just spoon the purée into individual glasses and pipe whipped cream around the edge. Again, Continental-style biscuits make a good accompaniment. Or use the purée as a delicious, emergency ice cream topping.

Home Economics is all about knowing what is available to make kitchen life more convenient in a busy schedule. Shop around and test out some non-perishable foods which may be unfamiliar. Finding your particular favourites and keeping a variety in stock will enable you to prepare lots of interesting meals in the shortest possible time.

Store Cupboard Stock List
Vegetable oil
Olive oil
Sesame seed oil
Vinegar – red wine
        white wine
        raspberry
Stock cubes
Yeast extract
Worcestershire sauce
Soy sauce
Tabasco sauce
Cranberry sauce
Mustard powder
Mustard seeds
French mustard
Wholegrain mustard
Black peppercorns
Green peppercorns in brine

Salt
Crushed chillies
Chilli powder
Hot pepper or chilli sauce
Mexican chilli seasoning
Cayenne pepper
Paprika pepper
Ground coriander
Coriander seeds
Fenugreek seeds
Sesame seeds
Ground cumin
Ground ginger
Garam masala
Dried mixed herbs
Curry powder
Curry paste
Tomato ketchup
Black olives
Sun-dried tomatoes

CANS
Vegetables – chopped tomatoes
             sweetcorn
             celery
             asparagus
             artichokes
             chick peas
             mushrooms
Beans – red kidney
        aduki
        flageolet
        red-brown
        borlotti
        cannelloni
Fish/Meat – Tuna in oil
            Salmon
            Ham
            Corned beef

Soups – condensed mushroom
         condensed tomato rice
         condensed chicken
         cream of tomato
Fruit – Lychees
        Black cherries
        Mango
        Melon
        Pineapple chunks
        Pineapple rings
        Crushed pineapple
        Mandarin oranges
Custard (ready made)
Dried fruit – Apricots
             Peaches
             Apples

DRY FOOD
Pasta – Tagliatelle
        Noodles
        Spaghetti
        Twists/bows/tubes
Cannelloni
Rice – Basmati
       Wild
       Brown
       Saffron
       Pilau
Lentils – Red
          Green/Continental
Bulgar Wheat
Instant potato
Naan bread mix
Dried mushrooms
Onions
Garlic
Nuts – Walnuts
       Flaked almonds
       Cashew nuts

16

Vacuum-packed chestnuts
Packet sauce mixes – White
                      Onion
                      Hollandaise
                      Bolognese
Packet stuffing mixes – Parsley and thyme
                        Herb and garlic
Chestnut purée
Soft brown sugar
Demerara sugar
Clear honey
Orange marmalade
Lime marmalade
Jams
Golden syrup
Peanut butter
Vanilla essence
Plain chocolate
Gelatine
Flour
Breadcrumbs
Desiccated coconut
Sultanas
Icing sugar
Sponge fingers
Continental-style biscuits – Amaretti
                             Wafers
                             Ratafias
                             Langues du chat
Melba toast

Fridge Stores
Although it is advisable to buy perishable foods regularly, the fridge can be stocked with a few longer-lasting ingredients which are useful in knocking up a quick meal.

Cheese: Feta and Parmesan last for several weeks and a tub of grated Parmesan is especially useful for flavouring pasta meals and sprinkling over food in a sauce prior to grilling. Cheddar and other similar hard cheeses last in good condition for a couple of weeks.

Mayonnaise: A jar of French-style mayonnaise, and perhaps one or two mayonnaise-based dressings are a must. Flavours include Avocado and Smoked Ham, Mild Curry, Garlic and Herb and Chilli and Avocado. Any one is ideal for turning a mundane salad into a bistro-style extravaganza. (See Avocado and Bacon Salad, page 186.)

Eggs: Eggs will keep for about 2 weeks, and half a dozen or so will always provide an instant omelette when time and energy are short.

Suet: Quick tasty casseroles can often be made from a variety of left-overs, or odds and ends of vegetables. A packet of shredded suet is useful to keep in the fridge for adding bulk and interest to such dishes. Vegetarian nut suet is available from health food shops.

Root Ginger: Fresh ginger keeps well in the fridge and is a useful flavouring for stir-fries and desserts.

Vacuum-packed Salami and Pepperoni: These highly flavoured cooked meats are wonderful for pizza-type toppings, pasta sauces and snacks.

Tomato Purée: Keep a tube tucked away in the fridge. It is indispensable for adding flavour and colour to sauces and casseroles.

Garlic and Herb butter: Again available in tubes it is most useful for tossing through freshly cooked pasta or making your own quick garlic bread.

Jif Lemon: A plastic lemon filled with juice is the answer when there are no fresh lemons in stock. Also less wasteful when a recipe calls for 'a squeeze' of lemon juice.

3   MAKE IT SNAPPY

No matter how simple a recipe is, inevitably there has to be some preparation otherwise it wouldn't be a recipe! And this means time chopping, time grating, time making a salad and time cooking vegetables and other accompaniments to a meal.

There are a few short cuts which can make life easier. Vegetables don't have to be cooked to death. Break the habits of a lifetime and simmer in a little water until just tooth-tender – the French have been doing it for years!

Alternatively don't cook vegetables at all – serve crudités instead. These are a selection of raw crunchy and healthy vegetables such as carrots, celery, cucumber, tomatoes, cauliflower, courgettes, mushrooms, fennel and radishes. Simply cut the vegetables into small florets, matchsticks or slices and either serve plain or trickled with vinaigrette dressing or with a tasty dip.

Crudités make a good accompaniment to many meat and fish dishes and also the type of light suppers featured in the Television Snacks chapter.

When planning meals it saves time and effort if you think in terms of two or three days at a time. Prepare a selection of crudités in one go and store in the fridge in a container with a tight-fitting lid.

Salad greens can be kept in the same way. To prolong the life of lettuce and watercress, cut a sliver off the stalk (watercress can be done a bunch at a time) and hold the head under cold running water for a few seconds. Shake well and store in the fridge.

Don't waste precious minutes boiling away delicate flavours; hours spent in the kitchen are something every busy cook can do without!

The goodness in potatoes lies just beneath the skin, so boil small new potatoes in their jackets. Scrub with a nailbrush rather than scraping or peeling. Bake larger potatoes in the oven or microwave.

Save time by cooking two or three times the number of potatoes you need. On subsequent nights they can be chopped, mixed with finely chopped onion and a little mayonnaise and served cold, or sliced and sautéed.

Extra vegetables can be cooked in the same way and used for dishes like the Vegetable and Cheese Bake (see page 53).

Chopped onion and garlic are common ingredients in quick recipes and again it saves time to prepare a week's supply in one go. Chop a few onions and cloves of garlic but remember that such highly flavoured foods must be stored in containers with tightly fitted lids otherwise all other food in the fridge will be tainted.

Chopped parsley is useful for flavouring and garnish. As it stays fresher and greener than most other herbs, chop a couple of bunches at a time and keep in the fridge. It's a great relief to be able to take out a handful when required, rather than have to chop a little each time a recipe demands a tablespoon or two.

Grated cheese has a multitude of uses and although available ready-grated, it is an expensive way of buying. Instead grate a block of cheese in one go and store in a covered container in the fridge.

Many of the recipes are a complete meal in themselves; others include suggested accompaniments and time should be allowed for their preparation and cooking. Usually this can be done while the main dish is cooking.

4   WORKING TO A BUDGET

If you are having to feed yourself (and perhaps a family) on a tight budget, shop around. You will be amazed at the bargains to be had if you keep your eyes open! Although supermarkets are fairly competitive for basics like flour, margarine, milk and sugar, in my experience national chains are expensive for fresh produce, particularly meat, fruit and vegetables.

A short way from where I live in Bristol there is an excellent discount butcher and greengrocer, and similar shops have sprung up all over the country in recent years. Markets are another source of value-for-money produce.

With modern preserving and food production methods, and vast quantities of imported goods, just about anything is available all the year round. Although fruit and vegetables tend to be at their cheapest when in season (see pages 256–258), it pays to keep your eyes on shop displays because prices vary from day to day and shop to shop, with certain items being offered at prices you can't afford to miss.

A random example of some bargain buys which I regularly take advantage of includes bags of mixed peppers costing the same price usually charged for one; similar bags of aubergines; two cauliflowers for the price of one; and pound bags of mushrooms and tomatoes at half the cost you would expect to pay in a supermarket.

Good Butchers' Buys

Butchers' home-made sausages and sausagemeat knock spots off the commercially prepared kind and I've used these in all the sausage recipes (see chapter 10). Bags of bacon bits are cheap and ideal for recipes which demand chopped bacon. Any excess can be frozen in small lots for future use.

I usually find that most cuts of meat cost less from a butcher but it's worth checking prices yourself before buying. For example, look for supermarket meat marked 'reduced price' and 'special offer' and look in freezer cabinets for value-for-money pork steaks, New Zealand lamb and other meaty bits and pieces.

Tips To Stay Within Budget

Most people decide what to eat and then do the shopping. Yet by planning in reverse you will have more chance of keeping within budget. If, for example, you spot a bargain at the butcher or greengrocer, snap it up and then find a recipe to fit. Likewise look in your fridge/freezer/store cupboard each week to see what needs eating up and then find a recipe which uses those particular ingredients.

No Excuse For Wastage

If any oddments are in danger of ending up in the bin, use them first! Add the remains of a bag of sultanas to scones, a rice salad or a curry; chop a couple of bacon rashers into an omelette; peel the skin off a shrivelled apple and slice the flesh into a salad; use up odd vegetables in soups and stews and if, like mine, the remnants of your soft brown sugar have formed a solid block, melt it down for Flapjacks (see page 221).

Store Cupboard Flavourings

Although you may need to keep occasional, and often expensive, flavourings to a minimum I do recommend keeping a

few multi-purpose items which are useful for adding flavour and interest to cheap meals. These include mayonnaise, tomato purée, yeast extract, stock cubes, a few
spices, Worcestershire sauce and a tub of grated Parmesan
cheese.

After the initial outlay, your weekly budget should gradually balance out because it is unlikely that everything will run
out at once. I find it's cheaper to buy loose spices from a
specialist shop and then fill my own jars, rather than buying
pre-packed jars from supermarkets.

Money-Off Coupons

I used to consider these an enormous nuisance until I added
up just how much money I was chucking in the bin! I now
study my junk mail a bit more carefully. The average
household receives a startling amount of money in special
offers during the year so, if you use the products, use the
coupons!

Christmas Clubs

Many butchers now run a savings plan to spread the cost of
meat at Christmas. Fifty pence or so paid in a week could be
worth thinking about.

Cash In On The Fruit Glut

On a warm summer weekend take the family on a pick-your-
own-fruit trip. Children will love it, especially sneaking the
odd strawberry out of the collection basket when they think
no one is looking!

June and July are the best months to catch cheap home-
grown strawberries, raspberries, redcurrants, blackcurrants,
gooseberries and many varieties of vegetable. In autumn
come blackberries (free from hedgerows!), tomatoes, plums
and cooking apples.

An hour or so spent picking will certainly save money;
prices are about half the shop rate. Alternatively, a drive into
the country or even into the leafier suburbs will lead to any
number of people selling, or almost giving away, fruit and
vegetables at their gates.

Frozen Assets

Freezing your crop (if you possess a freezer) will set you up for the months ahead when fresh produce is expensive and scarce.

Raspberries, blackberries, gooseberries, blackcurrants, redcurrants and sliced cooking apples (peeled and cored first) all freeze well. For best results, freeze separately on baking trays and, when hard, pack into individual polythene bags.

Strawberries tend to go mushy if frozen and are best frozen as a purée and used to make ice cream, sorbet and sauces. Tomatoes too are best frozen as a sauce (see page 71 for Fresh Tomato Sauce).

Grow Your Own Herbs

I have already recommended the use of fresh herbs and that you grow your own by the kitchen door. For the cost of one bunch from the supermarket you can enjoy an almost permanent supply. Nothing compares with the flavour of fresh herbs and they need little space to grow. A few pots or a window box are all that's required.

Buy healthy plants from a nursery or specialist grower who will be happy to advise on planting and uses. As a general suggestion, start with a few of the more common and useful varieties – parsley, basil, mint, rosemary, chives and sage.

And Finally

Try to allocate a certain amount of money each week for food and restrict yourself to this budget. If you've been relying heavily on ready-prepared items you may not manage it at first. Start by making one or two of the basic essential recipes (see chapter 16, Back to Basics). Shopping is habit-forming and eventually, with a little perseverance, you'll forget all about convenience foods. Finally, don't get tempted with non-essentials and never shop when you're hungry!

5 ABOUT THE RECIPES

In terms of workload and financial restraints, the average woman who is juggling her job with her family is probably the hardest hit by the demands of after work cooking. For this reason the recipes – bar one or two – are designed to serve two adults and two children.

Yet there comes a time when even the bed-sit dweller, who relies on take-aways, and the executive who dines out, yearns for a home-cooked meal.

The experienced cook will no doubt work out his or her own ways of adapting the recipes to serve fewer people. Juggling ingredients and gauging quantities comes with experience, or trial and error. As a general guide, the recipes which are the easiest to adapt to single servings are those which won't leave you with loads of left-overs.

Here are some examples:

Mexican Honeyed Chicken (page 168) – For a single serving use two or three chicken thighs and make the glaze with 1 tablespoon of honey and half a teaspoon of chilli powder.

Devilled Chicken Drumsticks (page 174) – For a single serving use about two drumsticks and make up the marinade with 1 tablespoon of oil, a shake of paprika and ginger and half a teaspoon of mustard powder. If, when you come to make the dish again, a more distinctive flavour is preferred, simply add more of the spices.

Eggs Duchesse (page 37) – For a single serving use 2 eggs, 1 tablespoon of milk, 1 tablespoon of dried mushrooms, 1 slice of ham and a knob of butter the size of a hazelnut.

Spaghetti Provençal (page 69) – For a single serving use 1 small onion, 1 courgette, omit the leeks, 1 oz (25g) mushrooms, half a tablespoon of oil, 2-3 oz (50-75g) spaghetti, and substitute the can of tomatoes with 2 chopped fresh tomatoes, a squeeze of tomato purée and a dash of water.

Honey and Mustard Glazed Lamb (page 146) – For a single serving use one lamb chop and a glaze made with half a teaspoon of honey and half a teaspoon of French mustard.

Another way of adapting a recipe is to cook enough of the main ingredient – usually meat, poultry, fish or pasta – to serve one or two people, but stick to the quantities given for the other ingredients. (That way you won't be left with half cans and cartons of perishables which invariably get thrown out.) Put the excess mixture or sauce in a small container and freeze it for future use. Even the ice compartment of a fridge will do. Time and energy are saved, because when you next fancy the same meal, all you have to do is cook the main ingredient.

Recipes which adapt well to this method include Turkey Capparis (page 169), Tandoori Chicken (page 171), Pork Royale (page 134), Tagliatelle in Spicy Tomato Sauce (page 63), Spaghetti Provençal (page 69), Pasta Niçoise (page 74), Store Cupboard Spaghetti Bolognese (page 68), Bacon Chops with Creamy Mushrooms (page 129), Gammon Marsala (page 132) and Gammon with Plum Relish (page 132).

If you have a freezer, probably the most hassle-free way of

cooking for one is to make up a complete recipe and freeze it in four individual dishes.

People cooking for two can of course halve the recipes exactly, unless they have large appetites in which case it might not be necessary! If you choose a recipe where you will be left with half cans and half cartons etc. look for other recipes which use the same ingredients.

For example:

Monday: Creamy Noodles (page 62) using half a carton of double cream.

Tuesday: Ratatouille (page 46) using half a can tomatoes, half an aubergine and half the peppers.

Wednesday: Pork Royale (page 134) using the other half tomatoes and cream.

Thursday: Liver with Peppercorn Sauce (page 140) using half a carton of soured cream.

Friday: Tagliatelle with Spicy Aubergine (page 66) using the other half aubergine and soured cream.

Saturday: Kebabs using the other half peppers.

People cooking for themselves could also follow this method. Similar juggling can be done with other recipes, e.g. those which use whole fruit or tins of fish when you only need half at a time. By planning out a couple of weeks' meals at a time you need never end up with odd bits and pieces.

To avoid unnecessary and time-consuming weighing, wherever possible, tablespoon (abbreviated tablsp) and teaspoon (abbreviated teasp) measurements are used. As a general guide use rounded spoonfuls, except in the case of flavourings when you may like to add more or less according to personal taste.

Technically there are no strict rules as to whether you use

plain or self-raising flour for thickening sauces and gravies. However self-raising may produce a more salty flavour – albeit minuscule – because of the raising agents it contains. I have always used whatever is to hand, with good results, including cornflour and brown flour.

Recipes are given in both imperial and metric measurements and for accuracy you should be consistent as to which one you use. Preparation and cooking times are approximate. Human nature, being what it is, means that some people work quicker than others; oven temperatures too can vary considerably.

Glossary of Culinary Terms

Basmati Rice – a rice grown at the foot of the Himalayas with long, slim grains. More expensive than other long-grained rice but considered to be the best.

Baste – to moisten meat, poultry or fish by spooning over juices from the dish while cooking.

Caramelise – obtain a brown syrupy mixture by boiling sugar in a liquid.

Dice – to cut into small cubes.

Escallop – a very thin slice of meat. Usually applies to veal although turkey escallops are now available.

Fold – a gentle stirring action to combine a whisked or creamed mixture with other ingredients so that it retains its lightness.

Fromage Frais – a soft cheese produced by introducing an acid-making culture to warm pasteurised skimmed milk which causes the milk to curdle. The curd is separated from the whey to produce the finished cheese. Many fruit-flavoured varieties of this popular cheese are now available.

Garam Masala – a combination of pungent ground mixed spices used in Indian cookery. Ready-mixed versions are available from large supermarkets and delicatessens.

Garnish – an edible savoury decoration such as parsley.

Kebab – cubes of marinaded meat, poultry or fish grilled on a skewer.

Liquor – the liquid in which meat, fish or vegetables is cooked.

Mange-tout – tiny peas in the pod which are eaten whole. Sometimes known as sugar peas.

Marinade – a blend of seasonings, spices and liquid such as wine, oil and vinegar which is used to soak meat prior to cooking.

Medallions – small rounds of meat.

Melba Toast – thin crisp slices of toasted bread. Also available in packets from the dry biscuit section of supermarkets.

Par-boil – boiling vegetables until they are partly cooked then finished off by some other method.

Poach – cooking gently in an open pan of simmering liquid. Usually applied to fish and eggs.

Reduce – the process of boiling a liquid in an uncovered pan in order to evaporate surplus liquid and give a more syrupy result.

Sauté – to fry gently in a little fat or oil.

Scant – just under the stated measurement.

Score – making shallow cuts on the surface of food.

Simmer – keeping a liquid at just below boiling point.

Soured Cream – made from fresh cream which has been commercially treated, rather like yoghurt, to give it a special flavour and texture. Soured cream is not as rich as ordinary cream and is ideal for both savoury and sweet dishes.

Vinaigrette Dressing – a mixture of one part vinegar to two parts oil and sometimes flavoured with herbs and spices.

Vol-au-Vent – a round or oval case made of puff pastry and filled with a sweet or savoury mixture. Ready-made frozen vol-au-vents are available at larger supermarkets.

Yeast Extract – a concentrated flavouring for savoury dishes. In the vegetarian diet it replaces meat stock cubes. Marmite is probably the best known brand but others are widely available.

6 EGGS AND CHEESE

EGGS

There is hardly a more versatile food than an egg. A good source of protein, vitamins, fat and minerals, eggs are quick to cook in a multitude of ways, making everything from simple snacks to substantial meals. They are suitable for sweet and savoury dishes and are used in most cakes and many hot and cold desserts. Moreover, compared to meat and fish, eggs are cheap. Half a dozen or so and a few bits and pieces and you have a nutritious, economical and filling meal for four.

Check butchers' prices before buying; they're often cheaper than supermarkets'.

Eggs are graded according to size with sizes 2 and 3 probably being the most useful in general cookery.

To separate an egg: Some recipes demand that the yolks and whites are added separately to other ingredients. For example in soufflés, in some batters and in meringue where only the whites are used.

Crack the egg smartly against the side of a bowl and then,

holding it over the bowl, break the shell in half holding the cracked sides up. Pass the yolk back and forth between the two shells; the white will drop into the basin and the yolk can be popped into a cup.

CHEESE

Cheese varies greatly in price, texture and flavour but generally speaking most varieties are an economical, nutritious and useful ingredient in basic cookery. Store cheese in a cool, airy place, lightly wrapped.

SPANISH OMELETTE   *Serves 4*

Omelettes are a favourite stand-by for an economical and quick meal. To make the dish more substantial you can add almost anything – grated cheese, fried mushrooms, prawns, chopped tomato, diced ham, spicy sausage and corn – or try a combination of several. A Spanish omelette is made differently from the others, more like a pancake. When it is cooked, serve cut in wedges with salad and fried matchstick potatoes. Omelettes are also good served with ratatouille (see page 46).

Preparation time: 8 mins.   *Cooking time: 25 mins.*

1 onion, peeled and chopped
1 small potato, peeled and diced
1 courgette, sliced
1 tablsp cooking oil
2 tomatoes, chopped
6 eggs
2 tablsp water
Salt and pepper

1. Heat the grill.

(continued overleaf)

2. Fry the onion, potato and courgette in the oil for about 15 minutes until tender.

3. Stir in the tomatoes.

4. Beat the eggs, water and seasoning together and pour into the vegetables. Cook for about 5 minutes until the eggs are brown and set on the underside.

5. Pop the frying pan under the grill and cook for a few minutes until the omelette is golden. Serve immediately.

OMELETTE MARGUERITA   *Serves 4*

Surprisingly this is quite a substantial meal and is good served with salad and fresh bread.

Preparation time: 10 mins.   *Cooking time: 15 mins.*

2 tablsp oil
4 spring onions, sliced
4 oz (100g) mushrooms, sliced
4 oz (100g) sliced salami
6 size 2 eggs, beaten
3 tablsp milk
Salt and freshly ground black pepper
2 oz (50g) Cheddar cheese, grated

1. Heat the oil in a large frying pan and sauté the spring onions and mushrooms for 8 minutes until tender.

2. Cut each slice of salami into 4 pieces, add to the pan and fry gently for a couple of minutes.

3. Pre-heat the grill to medium.

4. Mix the beaten eggs, milk and seasoning together and pour into the frying pan.

5. Cook over a gentle heat until the mixture half-sets then sprinkle on the cheese.

6. Pop the frying pan under the grill for a few minutes until golden brown and puffy. Cut into wedges and serve immediately.

HALLOUMI PAN FRY   *Serves 4*

This quick recipe is a type of omelette from Cyprus which was given to me by George, who is now living in the U.K. Halloumi is Cypriot cheese made with sheep's milk, which rather resembles Mozarella in flavour and texture though not as stringy. It is available from specialist shops but you could substitute other cheese. Serve with tomato salad and sesame seed bread.

Preparation time: 5 mins.   *Cooking time: 15 mins.*

1 small onion, peeled and chopped
2 tablsp olive oil
4 oz (100g) Halloumi cheese, sliced
Small bunch flat leaf parsley, roughly chopped
Few black olives, stoned
6 eggs
Salt and pepper
1 tablsp water

1. Fry the onion in the oil for about 10 minutes until tender.

2. Push the onion to one side and add the cheese, frying for a few minutes until each side is brown.

3. Add the parsley and olives, stirring over a low heat for a couple of minutes to mix the ingredients.

4. Beat the eggs, seasoning and water together and pour into the pan.

(continued overleaf)

5. As the egg cooks around the sides, draw it into the centre letting the uncooked egg run underneath. When the mixture has set like an omelette, cut into four wedges and serve.

CHEESE SOUFFLÉ   *Serves 2*

This makes a tasty, yet cheap, light lunch or supper dish. Serve with salad and garlic bread.

Preparation time: 10 mins.   *Cooking time: 20 mins.*

1 oz (25g) margarine
1½ level tablsp flour
½ level teasp dry mustard
¼ pt (150ml) milk
3 oz (75g) mature Cheddar cheese, grated
3 size 3 eggs, separated
Salt and freshly ground black pepper
Few chopped fresh chives (optional)

1. Pre-heat oven to 180°C (350°F) or Gas No 4.

2. Grease two individual soufflé dishes, 4" (10.2cm) in diameter or one dish about 6" (15.2cm).

3. Melt the margarine in a medium sized saucepan, add the flour and mustard and stir over a low heat to make a thick glossy paste.

4. Gradually stir in the milk; bring to the boil, stirring all the time until the sauce has thickened.

5. Add the grated cheese and stir until melted.

6. Now beat in the egg yolks one by one, using a wooden spoon.

7. Season with salt and pepper and stir in the chives if using.

8. In a bowl, whisk the egg whites until stiff then, using a metal spoon, fold the whites into the cheese mixture.

9. Pour into the prepared dishes or dish and bake for 15-20 minutes until the soufflés are well risen and golden.

Tip: These make an economical and unusual starter for a dinner party.

SPINACH ROULADE WITH CREAMY MUSHROOM FILLING   *Serves 4*

A roulade is similar to a soufflé in texture but made flat in a Swiss roll tin and then rolled around a filling. I particularly like the combination of spinach and creamy mushrooms in this recipe. Serve with a potato salad or fresh crusty bread and butter. For best results, eat the roulade as soon as possible after cooking.

Preparation time: 25 mins.   *Cooking time: 12 mins.*

1½ lb (700g) spinach
4 size 2 eggs
Salt and freshly ground black pepper
2 oz (50g) margarine
6 oz (175g) mushrooms, sliced
1 oz (25g) flour
4 fl oz (120ml) milk
Grated Parmesan cheese

1. Pre-heat oven to 200°C (400°F) or Gas No 6.

2. Grease and line a Swiss roll tin or baking tray about 8" × 12" (20.5cm × 30cm).

(continued overleaf)

3. Discard any very coarse stalks from the spinach, wash the leaves and then cook without using extra water until just tender, about 8 minutes. Drain then chop finely.

4. Separate the eggs, putting the whites into a large bowl.

5. Stir the yolks into the spinach and season with salt and pepper.

6. Whisk the egg whites until they are stiff enough to stand in soft peaks.

7. Very lightly fold the whites into the spinach mixture.

8. Pour the mixture into the prepared tin and bake for 12-15 minutes until lightly brown and firm to the touch.

9. Meanwhile, melt the margarine in a small saucepan and gently fry the mushrooms for 8 minutes.

10. Stir in the flour and cook for 1 minute.

11. Gradually stir in the milk. Bring to the boil and stir for a couple of minutes until the mixture thickens.

12. Have ready a damp tea towel, doubled and laid flat on a work surface. Lay a sheet of greaseproof paper on top and sprinkle with a little grated Parmesan cheese. (The damp tea-towel creates steam when the hot roulade is turned out, thus minimising it cracking when being rolled up.)

13. Turn the roulade out on to the greaseproof paper and peel off the lining paper.

14. Spread on the mushroom mixture to within 2" (5cm) of the edge.

15. Roll up the roulade like a Swiss roll, using the grease-proof paper to help ease it into shape.

EGGS DUCHESSE

Serves 4

A rather grand name for glorified scrambled eggs! It is particularly good served on squares of crispy fried bread – naughty but nice! (For a single serving use 2 eggs, 1 tablespoon of milk, 1 tablespoon of dried mushrooms, 1 slice of ham and a knob of butter the size of a hazelnut.)

Preparation time: 15 mins.   *Cooking time: 10 mins.*

**Handful of dried sliced mushrooms OR fresh sliced
   mushrooms**
6 eggs
3 tablsp milk
Salt and pepper
4 oz (100g) cooked ham, diced
Large knob butter

1. Put the dried mushrooms in a cup and pour on boiling water. Leave for 15 minutes then drain.

2. Beat the eggs, milk and seasoning together and add the diced ham and drained, dried mushrooms (or the fresh sliced mushrooms, if using).

3. Melt the butter in a small saucepan, pour in the egg mixture and cook gently like scrambled eggs, stirring continuously.

CHEESE AND ONION FLAN

Serves 4

A simple flan which is good served with jacket potatoes and salad.

Preparation time: 15 mins.   *Cooking time: 45 mins.*

2 onions, peeled and chopped
1 tablsp oil
4 oz (100g) short crust pastry (half the recipe on
   page 234 or frozen, defrosted)
3 oz (75g) tasty Cheddar cheese, grated
2 size 2 eggs, beaten
Approx. ¼ pt (150ml) milk
Salt and freshly ground black pepper

1. Fry the onions in the oil for about 15 minutes until lightly brown.

2. Meanwhile, make the pastry according to instructions on page 234 (halving the ingredients) or take the defrosted pastry and continue as below.

3. Roll out and use to line an 8" (20.5cm) flan ring or sandwich tin.

4. Pre-heat oven to 200°C (400°F) or Gas No 6.

5. Put the drained onions and grated cheese in the pastry case.

6. Beat the eggs in a measuring jug and make up to ½ pt (300ml) with milk. Season with salt and pepper.

7. Strain the egg mixture into the pastry case and bake for about 30 minutes until well risen and golden brown.

QUICHE LORRAINE

Serves 4

Home-made quiches are much crisper and tastier than the often soggy bought varieties. Serve this inexpensive supper with jacket or new potatoes and salad.

Preparation time: 15 mins.   *Cooking time: 30 mins.*

4 oz (100g) streaky bacon OR bacon bits
6 oz (175g) short crust pastry (see page 234
   or use frozen, defrosted)
2 oz (50g) tasty Cheddar cheese, grated
2 size 2 eggs, beaten
½ pt (300ml) milk
Salt and freshly ground black pepper

1. Pre-heat oven to 200°C (400°F) or Gas No 6.

2. Grill the bacon until crisp and then cut into pieces.

3. Meanwhile, make the pastry as per page 234 but use 6 oz (170g) of flour and 3 oz (75g) margarine only, or take the defrosted pastry and continue as below.

4. Roll out the pastry and use to line an 8" (20.5cm) flan ring or sandwich tin.

5. Put the bacon and cheese in the pastry case.

6. Beat the eggs, milk, salt and pepper together and strain through a sieve into the pastry case.

7. Bake for about 30 minutes until the filling is brown and firm to the touch.

BLUE CHEESE QUICHE

Serves 4

Traditionally Roquefort cheese is used but as it is the most expensive of the blue cheeses, alternatives such as Danish Blue or Bleu D'Auvergne are cheaper and work well. Served immediately after cooking, this quiche has a soufflé-like texture but it is also delicious cold when the texture is more solid like a cheesecake. Jacket potatoes and a salad are good accompaniments.

Preparation time: 20 mins.   *Cooking time: 30 mins.*

6 oz (175g) short crust pastry (see page 234, or use frozen, defrosted)
5 oz (125g) Bleu D'Auvergne or Danish Blue cheese
4 oz (113g) carton cream cheese
2 size 2 eggs, beaten
¼ (150ml) milk
Few chopped chives OR 1 small onion, finely chopped

1. Pre-heat oven to 200°C (400°F) or Gas No 6.

2. Make the pastry as per page 234 but use only 6 oz (175g) flour and 3 oz (75g) margarine, or take the defrosted pastry and continue as below.

3. Roll out the pastry and use to line an 8" (20.5cm) flan ring or sandwich tin.

4. Cream the cheeses together until well blended and then beat in the eggs and milk.

5. Finally stir in the chives or onion and pour the mixture into the pastry case.

6. Bake for about 15 minutes and then turn the oven down to 180°C (350°F) or Gas No 4 and cook for a further 15 minutes until the quiche is golden brown and puffy.

BACON AND EGG PIE

Serves 4

This is usually successful with children. It is just as good served hot with vegetables and potatoes as cold with salad.

Preparation time: 15 mins.   *Cooking time: 20 mins.*

6 oz (175g) smoked streaky bacon, diced
½ tablsp oil
3 eggs
3 tablsp milk
1 lb (450g) short crust (see page 234 or use frozen, defrosted)

1. Pre-heat oven to 220°C (425°F) or Gas No 7.

2. Fry the bacon in the oil for about 15 minutes until fairly crispy.

3. Beat the eggs and milk together.

4. Make the pastry as per page 234, using 1 lb (450g) flour and 8 oz (225g) margarine, unless using frozen, defrosted.

5. Roll out half the pastry and line a 10" (26cm) shallow tin plate. Sprinkle the bacon over the pastry and pour on all but a tablespoon of the egg mixture.

6. Using the reserved egg, brush the edges of the pastry. Roll out the remaining pastry and use to cover the pie. Press down firmly, pinch edges and brush the top with the reserved egg.

7. Bake in oven for about 12 minutes, then turn down oven to 170°C (325°F) or Gas No 3 for a further 8 minutes until well risen and golden.

CHEESE PLATE PIE

Serves 4

This is a shallow tin plate pie with a light and fluffy cheese filling. It is good hot or cold but is best eaten on the day of cooking. Serve with buttered new potatoes and salad.

Preparation time: 10 mins.   *Cooking time: 20 mins.*

2 oz (50g) butter or margarine
4 oz (100g) mature Cheddar cheese, grated
2 eggs, beaten
Salt and pepper
1 lb (450g) short crust pastry (see page 234 or
**   use frozen, defrosted)**

1. Pre-heat oven to 220°C (425°F) or Gas No 7.

2. Melt butter or margarine in a small saucepan, then stir in the grated cheese, beaten egg and seasoning.

3. Heat gently, stirring all the time, for about 5 minutes, until mixture thickens and coats the back of the spoon. Set aside to cool.

4. Meanwhile, make the pastry as per page 234 using 1 lb (450g) flour and 8 oz (225g) margarine, or take the defrosted pastry and continue as below.

5. Roll out half the pastry and line a 8 to 9" (20 to 23cm) tin pie plate. Trim edges.

6. Spread on the cheese mixture to within ½" (1.5cm) of the edge. Brush edges with beaten egg or milk.

7. Roll out remaining pastry and cover pie. Trim and pinch edges, brush the top with beaten egg or milk and bake for about 15 minutes until well risen and golden.

7   VEGETARIAN MEALS

Although these recipes are not aimed totally at the vegetarian, there are several in this chapter, and throughout the book, which satisfy this criterion. (See also chapters on Eggs and Cheese, Pasta, Grains and Pulses and Television Suppers, Snacks and Salads.)

However, whether for health, social or economical reasons, statistics show that more people are eating less meat. This section is therefore largely aimed at those who perhaps like to include a couple of meatless, or almost meatless, meals in their weekly menu.

Soya bean products, like tofu (which is available in varying textures), make a good alternative to meat and fish. Rich in protein, minerals and vitamins, tofu is both healthier and cheaper. It can be shallow and deep fried and marinaded and makes an ideal substitute for meat in many of the recipes in this book. Soya mince is also available and it is well worth keeping a couple of packets in stock for a store cupboard Bolognese sauce (see page 68).

BAKED TOMATOES WITH HERB AND CRUMB TOPPING

Serves 4

This is a convenient way of using up an autumn glut of tomatoes, or when shop prices are low. Serve with cold meat or a mixed bean salad and crusty rolls.

Preparation time: 6 mins.   *Cooking time: 15 mins.*

12 average sized tomatoes
Salt and pepper
1 teasp sugar
3 oz (75g) parsley and thyme stuffing mix
2 tablsp cooking oil

1. Pre-heat oven to 190°C (375°F) or Gas No 5.

2. Cut each tomato into three thick slices and arrange in an ovenproof dish.

3. Season with salt and pepper and sprinkle on the sugar.

4. Shake the dry stuffing mix evenly over the tomatoes and trickle over the oil.

5. Cook in oven for about 15 minutes until the topping is golden.

VEGETABLE CURRY

Serves 4

At first glance this recipe has a rather off-putting long list of ingredients, but it is a throw-it-all-in-the-pot meal and quite quick to prepare. Serve with pilau rice or naan bread.

Preparation time: 15 mins.   *Cooking time: 40 mins.*

1 teasp coriander seeds
2 teasp cumin
1 teasp garam masala
1 teasp mustard seeds
2 cloves garlic, peeled and finely chopped
6 tablsp cooking oil
1 large onion, peeled and chopped
2 fresh chillies, chopped OR 1 teasp crushed dried
  chillies
½ lb (225g) button mushrooms
1 aubergine, cut into dice
½ lb (225g) leeks, sliced
4 medium potatoes, peeled and cut into dice
1 cauliflower, broken into florets
14 oz (397g) can peeled tomatoes
1 teasp salt
Pepper

1. Pre-heat oven to 170°C (325°F) or Gas No 3.

2. Crush the coriander seeds with a rolling pin.

3. Sauté coriander, cumin, garam masala, mustard seeds and garlic in the oil for a couple of minutes.

4. Add all the remaining ingredients and sauté for about 10 minutes, stirring frequently.

5. Turn the mixture into an ovenproof casserole with lid and cook for about 30 minutes until the vegetables are tender. Adjust seasoning if necessary.

RATATOUILLE

Serves 4

This is a well-known, classic vegetable dish and has a flavour like no other. The Mediterranean aroma of garlic frying in olive oil is delicious in itself! Serve with hot garlic bread.

Preparation time: 12 mins.   *Cooking time: 30 mins.*

4 tablsp olive oil
2 onions, peeled and sliced
1 aubergine, diced
4 courgettes, sliced
4 tomatoes, cut into pieces
1 green pepper, de-seeded and sliced
1 red pepper, de-seeded and sliced
2 cloves garlic, peeled and finely chopped
2 tablsp tomato purée
Salt and pepper

1. Heat the oil in a large saucepan.

2. Add all the prepared vegetables, tomato purée and seasoning.

3. Stir over a low heat for 5 minutes, then put a lid on the saucepan and cook for a further 25 minutes. The vegetables should be soft and well blended but not pulpy.

MUSHROOM AND BROCCOLI PIE   *Serves 4*

Mushrooms, onion and broccoli combine with a thick gravy, flavoured with yeast extract and tomato purée, to make a tasty pie. Lightly cooked carrot sticks make a perfect accompaniment.

Preparation time: 10 mins.   *Cooking time: 20 mins.*

1 tablsp butter or margarine
8 oz (225g) mushrooms, sliced
1 onion, peeled and chopped
8 oz (225g) broccoli
¼ pt (150ml) water
1 tablsp flour
1 tablsp tomato purée
2 teasp yeast extract
8 oz (225g) short crust pastry (see page 234 or
  use frozen, defrosted)

1. Pre-heat oven to 220°C (425°F) or Gas No 7.

2. Melt the butter or margarine in a frying pan and sauté the mushrooms and onion for about 10 minutes until tender.

3. Meanwhile cut the broccoli into small florets and slice the stalks. Bring the ¼ pt (150ml) water to the boil, add the broccoli and simmer for five minutes. Drain and reserve the liquor.

4. Stir in the flour, tomato purée, yeast extract and broccoli water into the mixture in the frying pan. Stir over a low heat until thickened.

5. Add the broccoli and pour the mixture into an oval or circular pie dish.

6. Make the pastry as per page 234, or take the defrosted pastry and continue as below.

7. Roll out the pastry and cover the pie filling. If liked, brush with beaten egg or milk then bake for about 10 minutes until golden.

SPINACH CANNELLONI

Serves 4

If you can prepare this dish the evening before eating, the cannelloni will have softened and therefore only about 10 minutes' cooking time is needed.

Preparation time: 10 mins.   *Cooking time: 10-40 mins.*

1 lb (450g) frozen spinach, defrosted and drained
2 tablsp shelled whole hazelnuts
Salt and pepper
10 cannelloni
14 oz (397g) can chopped chilli tomatoes
7 oz (200g) feta cheese

1. Pre-heat the oven to 180°C (350°F) or Gas No 4.

2. Mix the spinach, nuts and seasoning together in a bowl and use the mixture to stuff the cannelloni.

3. Lay the cannelloni close together in a shallow ovenproof dish.

4. Pour over the tomatoes, together with a splash of boiling water.

5. Crumble the feta cheese over the top and bake for about 40 minutes. (If the dish is prepared beforehand, the cannelloni will soften and need less cooking time, as stated at the start of the recipe.)

AUBERGINE BAKE

Serves 4

A truly delicious dish as the cream and stock combine to complement the creamy texture of the vegetables. Serve with garlic bread.

Preparation time: 10 mins.   *Cooking time: 40 mins.*

2 onions, peeled and sliced
1 large aubergine, sliced thinly
8 oz (225g) mushrooms, sliced
Salt and pepper
1 tablsp flour
1 stock cube, made up with ¼ pt (150ml) water
5 fl oz (150ml) single cream
3 tablsp white wine OR water
3 oz (75g) commercially prepared brown breadcrumbs

1. Pre-heat oven to 190°C (375°F) or Gas No 5.

2. Layer half the onions, aubergine and mushrooms in a large ovenproof casserole.

3. Season well and sprinkle the flour over the vegetables. Layer the remaining vegetables on top, finishing with the aubergine.

4. Pour on the stock, cream and wine or water.

5. Sprinkle the breadcrumbs over and bake for about 40 minutes.

VEGETABLE INDIENNE   *Serves 4*

Subtly flavoured with a hint of lemon and ginger, these tooth-tender vegetables make a wonderful healthy supper dish. Vegetarians can omit the prawns and substitute bean sprouts and a few chestnuts. Serve with hot garlic bread.

Preparation time: 12 mins.   *Cooking time: 25 mins.*

4 tablsp cooking oil
1 onion, peeled and sliced
Large knob ginger, peeled and grated
12 oz (350g) broccoli, cut into small pieces
1 lb (450g) courgettes, sliced
1 red pepper, de-seeded and sliced
1 yellow pepper, de-seeded and sliced
8 oz (225g) mange-tout
2 teasp curry paste
Juice 1 lemon
1 teasp yeast extract, mixed with ¼ pt (150ml) water
8 oz (225g) peeled prawns

1. Heat the oil in a wok or very large frying pan; failing these a large saucepan will do.

2. Add the onion, ginger, broccoli, courgettes, peppers and mange-tout.

3. Stir-fry the vegetables for 15 minutes.

4. Stir in the curry paste, lemon juice, yeast extract and water. Cook gently for a further 10 minutes.

5. Add the prawns and serve garnished with chopped fresh coriander if liked.

MUSHROOM AND ASPARAGUS
VOL-AU-VENTS
Serves 4

Frozen ready-prepared vol-au-vents, which are made with puff pastry, are a great help to the busy cook. They come in three sizes – cocktail, medium and king-size. All manner of fillings can be devised to make a quick supper dish. (See also chapters on Fish, Meat, Television Suppers and Desserts.) Experiment with your own particular favourite combinations.

Preparation time: 8 mins.   *Cooking time: 17 mins.*

4 king-size frozen vol-au-vents
4 oz (100g) mushrooms, sliced
1 clove garlic, peeled and chopped
1 tablsp cooking oil
10.4 oz (295g) can condensed mushroom soup
Small can (12 oz/340g) cut asparagus or tips, drained
Ground black pepper

1. Pre-heat oven to 220°C (425°F) or Gas No 7. Cook the vol-au-vents in the oven for about 12 minutes until well risen and lightly brown.

2. Meanwhile fry the mushrooms and garlic in the oil for about 10 minutes until tender.

3. Put the soup in a bowl and mix in the drained mushrooms, garlic, asparagus and a good grind of black pepper.

4. Remove lids from the vol-au-vents and pull out uncooked pastry and discard.

5. Fill the vol-au-vents with the mushroom mixture – pop on the lids and heat in the oven for 5 minutes. Serve with new potatoes and salad.

CHESTNUT DHANSAK   *Serves 4*

Of Indian origin, this deliciously flavoured recipe traditionally uses lamb and lentils. Here the 'meat' is whole chestnuts,
making it ideal for vegetarians. If you can get to a delicatessen, the cooked dry, or vacuum-packed, chestnuts are the
closest in flavour and texture to the fresh nut. Canned whole
chestnuts are available from large supermarkets.

Preparation time: 10 mins.   *Cooking time: 25 mins.*

5 tablsp cooking oil
2 teasp coriander seeds, crushed
½ teasp chilli powder
1 teasp turmeric
1 teasp cumin
1 aubergine, cut into chunks
1 onion, peeled and chopped
4 oz (100g) red lentils
14 oz (397g) can chopped tomatoes
**15 oz (425g) whole chestnuts, drained but reserve liquor
  if canned**
12 oz (350g) spinach, washed and sliced
Salt and pepper
5 fl oz (150ml) carton natural yoghurt
Fresh coriander for garnish (optional)

1. Heat the oil in a large saucepan and add the next six
    ingredients.

2. Fry gently for 5 minutes, stirring well, then add the
    lentils, tomatoes, chestnuts and the liquor made up to
    ¼ pt (150ml) with water.

3. Pile the spinach on top with a generous shake of salt and
    pepper. Bring to the boil, put on a lid and simmer gently
    for 20 minutes, stirring occasionally.

4. Stir in the yoghurt and serve garnished with chopped
    coriander if liked.

5. Serve accompanied with brown rice or naan bread.

VEGETABLE AND CHEESE BAKE   *Serves 4*

A mixture of grated cheese and potato gives a tasty crunchy topping to vegetables in onion sauce. Use any combination of cooked vegetables but if none are to hand, a large packet of frozen broccoli, cauliflower and baby carrots gives excellent results.

Preparation time: 12 mins.   *Cooking time: 30 mins.*

1 pt (500ml) onion sauce (see page 250) OR 2 packets (standard/25g size) onion sauce mix (make ½ pt each) and 1 pt (500ml) milk
2 teasp mustard powder (optional)
Freshly ground black pepper
2 lb (907g) cooked mixed vegetables or frozen pack
2 large potatoes, peeled and coarsely grated
4 oz (100g) mature Cheddar cheese, grated

1. Pre-heat oven to 180°C (350°F) or Gas No 4.

2. Make the onion sauce as per page 250 using 2 oz (50g) flour, 2 oz (50g) margarine and 1 pt (500ml) milk, adding mustard powder, if using. Season with pepper.

    Alternatively:

    Empty the sauce mixes into a saucepan and add the mustard powder, if using. Make the sauce according to manufacturer's instructions with the milk. Season with pepper.

3. Stir the vegetables into the sauce and pour into an oven-proof dish.

4. Mix the potatoes and cheese together and arrange on top of the vegetables.

5. Bake for 30 minutes until the topping is brown and crispy.

(continued overleaf)

Tip: A variation on this recipe can be made by mixing cooked vegetables with a cheese sauce, but instead of the potato and cheese topping, split 4 croissants horizontally and use as a top and bottom 'pie crust'.

MUSHROOM DOPIAZZA   *Serves 2*

This is one of several recipes which I have adapted from similar commercially prepared examples – at one third of the price!

Preparation time: 10 mins.   *Cooking time: 20 mins.*

3 tablsp oil
12 oz (350g) mushrooms, thinly sliced
1 large onion, peeled and roughly chopped
1 clove garlic, peeled and finely chopped
Salt and freshly ground black pepper
1 teasp flour
1 teasp garam masala
2 teasp paprika
1 teasp cumin
1 teasp ground ginger
1 teasp coriander
14 oz (397g) can peeled tomatoes

1. Heat the oil in a large frying pan and gently cook the mushrooms, onion and garlic for 10 minutes.

2. Stir in the remaining ingredients, ending with tomatoes, and cook gently for a further 10 minutes before serving.

COURGETTES AND TOMATOES WITH BASIL

Serves 2

Make this tasty, light lunch or supper dish when courgettes reach rock bottom price, usually in June or July. Serve with fresh crusty bread and butter.

Preparation time: 10 mins.   *Cooking time: 10 mins.*

1 tablsp oil
1 lb (450g) courgettes, sliced
2 beefsteak tomatoes
Salt and freshly ground black pepper
2 tablsp roughly chopped fresh basil

1. Heat the oil in a saucepan or large frying pan and stir-fry the courgettes for 5 minutes.

2. Remove and discard the skins from the tomatoes by spearing with a fork and plunging into boiling water for a few seconds. Slice the flesh.

3. Add the tomatoes, salt, pepper and basil to the courgettes and continue stir-frying for a further 5 minutes until the courgettes are tender and the tomatoes have broken down.

TOMATO, BEAN AND CHEESE BAKE   *Serves 2*

Serve with garlic bread or brown rice.

Preparation time: 15 mins.   *Cooking time: 30 mins.*

2 onions, peeled and roughly chopped
1 lb (450g) runner beans, sliced
2 beefsteak tomatoes
Freshly ground black pepper
½ pt (300ml) basic white sauce (see page 249) OR 1
   packet (17g size) white sauce mix
4 oz (100g) Cheddar cheese, grated

1. Pre-heat the oven to 180°C (350°F) or Gas No 4.

2. Cook the onions and beans in boiling, salted water for about 10 minutes until just tender. Drain.

3. Peel the tomatoes by spearing with a fork and dipping in boiling water for a few seconds. Roughly chop the flesh.

4. Mix the onions, beans and tomatoes together and season with black pepper.

5. Make the sauce as per page 249, or follow manufacturer's instructions.

6. Stir the sauce into the vegetables and pour the mixture into a shallow ovenproof dish.

7. Top with grated cheese and bake for 20 minutes until the cheese is golden brown and bubbly.

SPICY VEGETABLE HOT POT   *Serves 4*

This is an ideal recipe for using up odd vegetables. Serve with plenty of fresh crusty bread or garlic bread.

Preparation time: 10 mins.   *Cooking time: 35 mins.*

2 tablsp oil
1 medium sized leek, sliced
1 medium sized courgette, sliced
1 medium sized carrot, sliced thinly
1 onion, peeled and chopped
4 oz (100g) button mushrooms
8 oz (225g) potatoes, peeled and diced
14 oz (397g) can peeled tomatoes
7.5 oz (220g) can red kidney beans, drained
½ pt (300ml) water
1 tablsp tomato purée
1 rounded teasp chilli powder
Salt and freshly ground black pepper
1 level tablsp cornflour or flour

1. Heat the oil in a saucepan and sauté the leek, courgette, carrot, onion and mushrooms for 5 minutes.

2. Meanwhile, par-boil (see page 29) the diced potatoes for 5 minutes. Drain and then add to the other vegetables.

3. Stir in the tomatoes, drained beans, water, tomato purée, chilli powder, salt and pepper.

4. Bring to the boil and then simmer gently, without a lid, for about 30 minutes until the vegetables are tender.

5. Mix the cornflour or flour with a little water and stir into the vegetable mixture. Boil up for a couple of minutes to thicken.

Tip: A more substantial dish can be made by turning the mixture into an ovenproof dish, topping with sliced cooked potato and sprinkling with a little grated cheese. Simply pop under the grill until brown and crispy.

CORN FRITTERS WITH FRESH TOMATO SAUCE

Serves 4

The tangy and juicy fresh tomato sauce perfectly offsets the richness of corn fritters, making a nutritious supper dish.

Preparation time: 20 mins.   *Cooking time: 43 mins.*

Fresh tomato sauce (see page 71)
¼ pt (150ml) fritter batter (see page 237)
11 oz (312g) can sweetcorn, drained

1. Make the tomato sauce as per page 71.

2. Make the batter as per page 237.

3. Stir the drained sweetcorn into the batter and deep fry teaspoonsfuls for 3-4 minutes. Drain on kitchen paper.

MEXICAN PANCAKES

Makes 8-10

Pancakes need moist fillings otherwise the overall dish will be too dry. This creamy tomato and mushroom stuffing, which is spiced 'hot' with chilli, is just the thing. Serve with boiled brown rice to give added texture.

Preparation time: 10 mins.   *Cooking time: 40 mins.*

½ pt (300ml) pancake batter (see page 236)
2 tablsp oil
1 onion, peeled and chopped
6 oz (175g) mushrooms, roughly chopped
12 oz (350g) tomatoes
1 tablsp tomato purée
2 oz (50g) packet cashew nuts (optional)
1 chilli, finely chopped
Salt and freshly ground black pepper
5 fl oz (142ml) carton soured cream

1. Make the pancake batter (see page 236).

2. Heat the oil and gently fry the onion and mushrooms until tender, about 12 minutes.

3. Meanwhile, skin the tomatoes by spearing with a fork and dipping in boiling water for one minute. The skin then easily peels off. Roughly chop the flesh.

4. Stir the tomato flesh, tomato purée, nuts (if using), chilli, salt, pepper and soured cream into the mushroom mixture and cook gently for a further 8 minutes.

5. Make and cook the pancakes as per stages 3 and 4 overleaf.

6. Divide the tomato mixture between the pancakes and roll up.

Tip: Unfilled pancakes can be cooked well in advance. They keep in the fridge for 2-3 days or they can be frozen by layering up the pancakes in between greaseproof paper and then wrapping the whole lot in foil. The pancakes will defrost in a very short time and can then be re-heated in a low oven.

SPINACH AND CREAM CHEESE PANCAKES

Serves 4

Serve with brown rice.

Preparation time: 15 mins.   *Cooking time: 40 mins.*

**½ pt (300ml) white or wholemeal pancake batter (see
     page 236)**
8 oz (225g) spinach
Little oil for frying
4 oz (100g) cream cheese
5 fl oz (150ml) carton soured cream
2 oz (50g) Cheddar cheese, grated

1. Make the pancake batter as per page 236. Leave to stand.

2. Wash and shred the spinach and cook in a little boiling
    water for 8 minutes until tender. Drain well.

3. Meanwhile, make the pancakes: Heat a teaspoon of oil in
    an 8" (20cm) frying pan and pour in just enough batter to
    cover the base thinly.

4. Cook for 2-3 minutes, then turn and cook the other side.
    Continue cooking the other pancakes in the same way.
    (The mixture makes about 8 pancakes.)

5. Pre-heat oven to 180°C (350°F) or Gas No 4.

6. Mix the spinach with the cream cheese and use the
    mixture to fill the pancakes.

7. Roll each pancake up and place in a shallow ovenproof
    dish.

8. Spoon over the soured cream and sprinkle with grated
    cheese.

9. Bake for about 10 minutes until the cheese has melted.

8   PASTA, GRAINS AND PULSES

PASTA

The number of quick and tasty sauces which can be made to create interesting pasta dishes is limited only by your imagination. All the following recipes can be prepared and cooked in less time than it takes to down a gin and tonic after a hard day's work! You'd pay a fortune for such a meal at an Italian restaurant!

Dried pasta, sold in packets, is the most commonly used. However, many people consider fresh pasta superior in flavour, and although more expensive, it is now available from large supermarkets and speciality shops.

Depending on appetite, allow between 2-3 oz (50-75g) of pasta per person. Dried varieties take about 8-10 minutes to cook, fresh takes less time. Cook in boiling salted water to which a little oil has been added. This prevents the pasta clogging together when cooked.

CREAMY NOODLES

Serves 4

Preparation time: 10 mins.   *Cooking time: 10 mins.*

8-12 oz (225-350g) noodles
Knob butter or margarine
6 oz (175g) mushrooms, sliced
6 oz (175g) ham, cut in strips
5 fl oz (150ml) double cream
2 oz (50g) mature Cheddar cheese, grated
1 tablsp milk

1. Cook the noodles in boiling salted water for about 8 minutes until tender.

2. Meanwhile, melt the butter or margarine in a frying pan and sauté the mushrooms for a few minutes until tender.

3. Add the ham, cream, cheese and milk and stir over a low heat until the cheese has melted.

4. Drain the noodles and toss through the sauce.

5. Serve sprinkled with chopped parsley if liked.

LEMON AND WALNUT TAGLIATELLE   *Serves 4*

This is a wonderfully healthy and fresh-looking pasta dish with crunchy nuts and courgettes in a tangy lemon cream sauce.

Preparation time: 12 mins.   *Cooking time: 15 mins.*

4 courgettes, cut into small dice
Grated rind and juice of 2 lemons
½ tablsp cooking oil
Knob butter or margarine
8-12 oz (225-350g) tagliatelle
Salt and pepper

2 tablsp walnut pieces
½ pt (300ml) single cream

1. Fry the courgettes and grated lemon rind in the oil and butter, or margarine, for about 10 minutes until tender.

2. Meanwhile cook the tagliatelle in boiling salted water for about 8 minutes.

3. Add seasoning, lemon juice and walnuts to the courgettes and when simmering, stir in the cream.

4. Drain the tagliatelle and fold through the sauce.

5. Garnish with chopped parsley if liked.

TAGLIATELLE IN SPICY TOMATO SAUCE

Serves 4

This mildly spiced sauce is delicious with pasta and is so quick and simple to make. (See page 26, for serving one or two.)

Preparation time: 5 mins.   *Cooking time: 12 mins.*

1 onion, peeled and chopped
1 tablsp cooking oil
8-12 oz (225-350g) tagliatelle
4 oz (100g) thinly sliced peppered salami
14 oz (397g) can chopped chilli tomatoes
Grated Parmesan cheese for garnish

1. Sauté the onion in the oil for about 10 minutes until soft.

2. Meanwhile cook the tagliatelle in boiling salted water for about 8 minutes until tender.

3. Cut the slices of salami into quarters and add to the onion. Fry gently for a couple of minutes.

(continued overleaf)

4. Stir in the chopped tomatoes and simmer for a further two minutes.

5. Drain the tagliatelle and fold through the sauce. Serve sprinkled with Parmesan cheese.

CHILLI PASTA   *Serves 4*

Cans of beans are now available in a mild chilli sauce. Give them a try in this quick and tasty supper dish.

Preparation time: 5 mins.   *Cooking time: 18 mins.*

1 large onion, peeled and chopped
4 oz (100g) mushrooms, sliced
2 tablsp oil
14 oz (400g) can red kidney beans in chilli sauce
14 oz (397g) can peeled tomatoes, drained
Salt and freshly ground black pepper
8 oz (225g) tagliatelle

1. Fry the onion and mushrooms gently in the oil for 10 minutes.

2. Stir in the beans, tomatoes, salt and pepper and simmer for 8 minutes.

3. Meanwhile, cook the tagliatelle in boiling, salted water for about 8 minutes until tender. Drain.

4. Divide the tagliatelle between 4 plates and top with the bean mixture.

BUTTERED TAGLIATELLE WITH BASIL AND MUSHROOMS

Serves 4

If you've followed my advice in Chapters 2 and 4, a nice clump of fresh basil should be growing in a pot! Don't be tempted to use dried herbs in this recipe; if necessary substitute parsley.

Preparation time: 10 mins.   *Cooking time: 20 mins.*

2 tablsp oil
8 oz (225g) mushrooms, sliced thinly
1 red pepper, sliced thinly
8-12 oz (225g-350g) tagliatelle
1 tablsp freshly chopped basil
Juice 1 lemon
Salt and freshly ground black pepper
3 oz (75g) butter or margarine
Grated Parmesan cheese

1. Heat the oil in a frying pan and sauté the mushrooms and red pepper for 10 minutes.

2. Meanwhile, cook the tagliatelle in boiling, salted water for about 12 minutes until tender. Drain.

3. Stir the basil, lemon juice, salt and pepper into the mushroom mixture and cook gently for a couple of minutes.

4. Return the drained tagliatelle to the saucepan and stir in the mushroom mixture and the butter.

5. Turn into a serving dish or individual plates and sprinkle with grated Parmesan cheese and plenty of freshly ground black pepper.

TAGLIATELLE WITH SPICY AUBERGINE *Serves 4*

Anyone who loves aubergine and the subtle spices of Indian food will adore this pasta sauce.

Preparation time: 10 mins.   *Cooking time: 15 mins.*

1 aubergine, cut into small dice
1 onion, peeled and chopped
½ teasp cayenne
1 teasp turmeric
1 teasp fenugreek seeds
Salt and pepper
4 tablsp cooking oil
8-12 oz (225-350g) tagliatelle
1 tablsp chopped fresh coriander
5 fl oz (150ml) carton soured cream

1. Fry the aubergine, onion, cayenne, turmeric, fenugreek seeds, salt and pepper in the oil for about 12 minutes until tender. Stir frequently during cooking.

2. Meanwhile cook the tagliatelle in boiling salted water for about 8 minutes.

3. Stir the coriander and soured cream into the aubergine mixture and heat for a couple of minutes.

4. Drain the tagliatelle and fold through the sauce.

BROCCOLI AND ROQUEFORT CREAM   *Serves 4*

This is a rich cream sauce highly flavoured with blue cheese, which goes well with a bland food such as pasta. Tiny florets of broccoli add colour and a crunchy texture.

Preparation time: 10 mins.   *Cooking time: 10 mins.*

8-12 oz (225-350g) tagliatelle
½ lb (225g) broccoli, cut into small florets
¼ pt (150ml) double cream
4 oz (100g) Roquefort, or other blue veined cheese
2 tablsp Greek yoghurt
Freshly ground black pepper

1. Cook the tagliatelle in boiling salted water for about 8 minutes.

2. Cook the broccoli in a little salted water for 3-4 minutes until just tender. Drain.

3. Put the cream in a small saucepan and crumble in the cheese. Heat gently until the cheese has melted.

4. Stir in the yoghurt, black pepper and broccoli.

5. Drain the tagliatelle and fold through the sauce.

STORE CUPBOARD SPAGHETTI BOLOGNESE

Serves 4

If shopping for fresh produce has been impossible, these store-cupboard ingredients make a tasty and filling meal which is also suitable for vegetarians. There is hardly any preparation necessary so the recipe is ideal for a late night impromptu supper. Soya products are available from health food shops and some supermarkets. (See page 26, for serving one or two.)

Preparation time: 3 mins.   *Cooking time: 15 mins.*

8 oz (225g) packet minced soya protein
14 oz (397g) can chopped tomatoes
Handful dried onion OR 1 peeled and chopped onion
Handful dried sliced mushrooms
Packet (standard/40g size) Bolognese sauce mix
   (makes ½ pint)
½ pt (300ml) water
8-12 oz (225-350g) spaghetti
Few black olives, stoned (optional)
Grated Parmesan cheese

1. Put the soya mince, tomatoes, onion, mushrooms and sauce mix in a saucepan.

2. Stir in the water, bring to the boil and simmer gently for 15 minutes.

3. Meanwhile cook the spaghetti in boiling salted water until tender, about 12 minutes. Drain.

4. If using olives, stir them into the Bolognese mixture.

5. Arrange the spaghetti on plates, pile the Bolognese mixture in the centre and serve with Parmesan cheese.

SPAGHETTI PROVENÇAL   *Serves 4*

This is a nice rich vegetable sauce to serve with spaghetti. Hot garlic bread makes a good accompaniment. (For a single serving use 1 small onion, 1 courgette, omit the leeks, 1 oz (25g) mushrooms, half a tablespoon of oil, 2-3 oz (50-75g) spaghetti, and substitute the can of tomatoes with 2 chopped fresh tomatoes, a squeeze of tomato purée and a dash of water.)

Preparation time: 10 mins.   *Cooking time: 15 mins.*

1 onion, peeled and chopped
3 courgettes, sliced
2 leeks, sliced
4 oz (100g) mushrooms, sliced
2 tablsp cooking oil
8-12 oz (225-350g) spaghetti
14 oz (397g) can tomatoes
1 tablsp chopped fresh oregano OR 1 teasp dried
Salt and freshly ground black pepper

1. Fry the onion, courgettes, leeks and mushrooms gently in the oil for about 15 minutes.

2. Meanwhile cook the spaghetti in boiling salted water for about 8 minutes.

3. Stir the tomatoes, herbs and seasoning into the vegetable mixture and cook for a couple of minutes.

4. Drain the spaghetti and fold through the sauce.

SPAGHETTI VERDE   *Serves 4*

This is simple and delicious but it is essential to use fresh herbs. Serve with a mixed salad.

Preparation time: 8 mins.   *Cooking time: 8 mins.*

2 cloves garlic, peeled and finely chopped
Small knob butter or margarine
8-12 oz (225-350g) spaghetti
Juice 1 lemon
2 tablsp chopped parsley
1 teasp each chopped rosemary, chives, chervil, basil and
**   oregano**
Butter
Freshly ground black pepper

1. Fry the garlic in the butter or margarine until tender.

2. Meanwhile cook the spaghetti in boiling salted water for about 8 minutes.

3. Add the lemon juice, parsley and herbs to the garlic and cook for a couple of minutes.

4. Drain the spaghetti and fold through the herb mixture, adding an extra knob of butter and some freshly ground black pepper.

SPAGHETTI CON FORMAGGIO   *Serves 4*

A dish of spaghetti, glistening with oil, is topped with a tasty mixture of crispy bacon, onions, mushrooms and cheese. Serve with garlic bread and salad.

Preparation time: 10 mins.   *Cooking time: 30 mins.*

8 oz (225g) streaky bacon, chopped
2 tablsp oil
1 onion, peeled and chopped

70

8 oz (225g) mushrooms, sliced
8-10 oz (225-275g) spaghetti
4 oz (100g) mature Cheddar cheese, grated
Extra oil

1. Fry the bacon for 10 minutes, then add the oil, onion and mushrooms and fry gently for a further 10 minutes.

2. Meanwhile, cook the spaghetti in boiling, salted water for about 8 minutes until tender.

3. Pre-heat grill to high.

4. Drain the spaghetti well, return to saucepan and toss in a good slug of oil until it glistens.

5. Pour the spaghetti into a shallow ovenproof dish and spoon the bacon mixture on top.

6. Top with grated cheese and grill under a high heat for a couple of minutes until golden brown.

SPAGHETTI WITH FRESH TOMATO SAUCE
Serves 4

Use ripe juicy tomatoes in this recipe. If the tomatoes are too firm, the sauce will be too thick in which case add a splash or two of water. Apart from serving with pasta, the sauce makes a wonderful accompaniment to fish cakes, meat loaves and sausages.

Preparation time: 15 mins.   *Cooking time: 40 mins.*

3 tablsp oil
1 onion, peeled and chopped
2 cloves garlic, peeled and finely chopped
1 lb (450g) ripe tomatoes
1 tablsp tomato purée

(continued overleaf)

SPAGHETTI WITH FRESH TOMATO SAUCE *continued*

Salt and freshly ground black pepper
1 bay leaf
8-12 oz (225-350g) spaghetti
1 tablsp freshly chopped basil
Grated Parmesan cheese (optional)

1. Heat the oil in a saucepan and gently fry the onion and garlic for 3-4 minutes.

2. Meanwhile, plunge the tomatoes into boiling water for a minute and then peel off and discard the skins. Roughly chop the flesh.

3. Add the tomatoes, tomato purée, salt, pepper and bay leaf to the onion and garlic.

4. Put a lid on the pan and cook very gently for 40 minutes. Stir the sauce occasionally, mashing the tomatoes against the side of the pan.

5. About 12 minutes before the sauce is ready, cook the spaghetti in boiling, salted water. Drain.

6. Remove the bay leaf from the sauce and stir in the chopped basil.

7. Tip the spaghetti into a serving dish or spoon on to individual plates and top with tomato sauce. Sprinkle with grated Parmesan cheese if liked.

Tip: In the autumn when tomatoes are at their cheapest, or if you spot a bargain bag at rock bottom price, make a bulk batch of sauce. Stored in a covered, rigid container, the sauce can be frozen for 2-3 months.

SPAGHETTI ALLA CARBONARA   *Serves 4*

A traditional Italian dish – spaghetti with bacon and eggs.

Preparation time: 10 mins.   *Cooking time: 15 mins.*

8 oz (225g) spaghetti
1 tablsp oil
8 oz (225g) smoked streaky bacon, diced
2 size 2 eggs, beaten
5 fl oz (142ml) single cream
Salt and freshly ground black pepper
Grated Parmesan cheese

1. Cook the spaghetti in boiling, salted water for about 12 minutes until tender. Drain.

2. Meanwhile, heat the oil and fry the bacon for about 10 minutes until crisp.

3. Beat the eggs, cream, salt and pepper and a little Parmesan cheese together.

4. Tip the spaghetti back into the pan, add the bacon and cream mixture and cook gently for 3 minutes. Turn into a serving dish and sprinkle with more Parmesan cheese.

BEEF CHOW MEIN   *Serves 4*

A very quick Anglicised – but tasty – version!

Preparation time: 10 mins.   *Cooking time: 15 mins.*

8 oz (225g) Chinese noodles or vermicelli
1 tablsp cooking oil
Juice 1 lemon
1 tablsp soy sauce

(continued overleaf)

2 teasp paprika
1 onion, peeled and chopped
2 cloves garlic, peeled and crushed
4 oz (100g) mushrooms, sliced
Handful frozen peas
7 oz (200g) can sweetcorn, drained
Small (8 oz/230g) can water chestnuts, sliced
12 oz (350g) rump steak, sliced thinly

1. Cook the noodles or vermicelli in boiling salted water until tender, about 8 minutes.

2. Meanwhile heat the oil, lemon juice, soy sauce and paprika in a large frying pan.

3. Add the onion, garlic, mushrooms, peas, sweetcorn and water chestnuts and cook gently for 8 minutes.

4. Add the steak and cook quickly for about 5 minutes, stirring all the time.

5. Fold the drained pasta through the meat mixture before serving.

PASTA NIÇOISE   *Serves 4*

There is a large selection of pasta shapes available, from bows, spirals and tubes to shells, wheels and alphabet letters. (See page 26 for serving one or two.)

Preparation time: 5 mins.   *Cooking time: 15 mins.*

1 clove garlic, peeled and finely chopped
1 onion, peeled and chopped
½ tablsp cooking oil
14 oz (387g) can chopped tomatoes
Salt and pepper

8-12 oz (225-350g) pasta shapes
7 oz (198g) can tuna fish in oil, drained

1. Fry the garlic and onion in the oil for a couple of minutes.

2. Stir in the tomatoes and seasoning and simmer for about 15 minutes until mixture has reduced slightly.

3. Meanwhile cook the pasta shapes in boiling salted water for about 8 minutes or until tender.

4. Stir the drained tuna fish into the tomato mixture and cook for a couple of minutes.

5. Drain the pasta and fold through the sauce. If liked, sprinkle with grated cheese.

SARDINE AND MACARONI GRILL   *Serves 4*

A tasty variation of macaroni cheese. Can be served on its own or with garlic bread and salad.

Preparation time: 10 mins.   *Cooking time: 20 mins.*

6 oz (175g) macaroni
2 oz (50g) margarine
4 oz (100g) mushrooms, sliced
1 oz (25g) flour
½ pt (300ml) milk
Salt and freshly ground black pepper
2 tomatoes, sliced
4.23 oz (120g) can sardines in oil, drained
2 oz (50g) mature Cheddar cheese, grated

1. Pre-heat grill.

2. Cook the macaroni in boiling, salted water for about 8 minutes until tender. Drain.

(continued overleaf)

3. Melt the margarine and fry the mushrooms for a few minutes until tender.

4. Stir in the flour and cook for 1 minute.

5. Gradually add the milk, stirring all the time. Bring to the boil and stir until thickened.

6. Season with salt and pepper and then stir in the macaroni.

7. Turn the mixture into a shallow ovenproof dish and top with the sliced tomatoes, lightly mashed sardines and grated cheese.

8. Pop under the grill for a few minutes until brown and bubbly.

MACARONI AND TUNA BAKE   *Serves 4*

Serve with garlic bread and salad or simply on its own.

Preparation time: 15 mins.   *Cooking time: 20 mins.*

6 oz (175g) macaroni
½ pt (300ml) white sauce (see page 249) or use 1 packet
  (17g size) white sauce mix
7 oz (185g) can tuna fish in oil, drained and flaked
4 oz (100g) frozen peas
3 oz (75g) tasty Cheddar cheese, grated

1. Pre-heat oven to 180°C (350°F) or Gas No 4.

2. Cook the macaroni in boiling, salted water for about 8 minutes until tender. Drain.

3. Meanwhile, make the white sauce according to instructions on page 249 or manufacturer's instructions on the packet.

4. Stir the macaroni, tuna and peas into the sauce and turn into a shallow ovenproof dish.

5. Sprinkle the cheese over the top and bake for about 20 minutes until brown and bubbly.

MOZZARELLA AND TOMATO QUILLS *Serves 3-4*

A deliciously simple and tasty supper dish. Serve with salad and garlic bread.

Preparation time: 15 mins.   *Cooking time: 10 mins.*

6 oz (175g) pasta quills or fat tubes
14 oz (397g) can peeled tomatoes, drained
2 tablsp oil
5 oz (150g) Mozzarella cheese, diced
2 tablsp freshly chopped basil
Salt and freshly ground black pepper
Grated Parmesan cheese

1. Cook the pasta in boiling, salted water until tender (about 10 minutes). Drain.

2. Pre-heat oven to 200°C (400°F) or Gas No 6.

3. Put the tomatoes and oil in a small saucepan and cook gently for 5 minutes, breaking up the tomatoes against the side of the pan.

4. Add the Mozzarella, basil, salt and pepper and heat gently for 1 minute.

5. Turn the pasta into a shallow ovenproof dish and pour over the sauce.

6. Sprinkle over some grated Parmesan cheese and bake for 10 minutes.

Tip: If you haven't got a pot of basil growing in your garden, substitute a can of chopped tomatoes with herbs for the peeled tomatoes and basil; it's cheaper than buying fresh basil for a one-off use.

SALMON PARISIENNE

Serves 4

A quick fork supper made with canned salmon, pasta and vegetables in a creamy wine and herb sauce. Serve with garlic bread.

Preparation time: 8 mins.   *Cooking time: 10 mins.*

6 oz (175g) thin cut macaroni or other pasta shapes
1 red pepper, de-seeded and chopped
4 oz (100g) fresh or frozen green beans
½ pt white sauce (see page 249) OR 1 packet (17g size)
  white sauce mix, made up with:
¼ pt (150ml) white wine } **or ½ pt (300ml) milk**
¼ pt (150ml) milk
14 oz (400g) can flageolet beans
15½ oz (440g) can salmon, drained and flaked
2 tablsp single cream (optional)
1 teasp chopped fresh dill (optional)
Salt and pepper

1. Cook the macaroni in boiling salted water for about 8 minutes until tender. Drain.

2. Cook the pepper and green beans in a little salted water for about 8 minutes until just tender.

3. Make up the sauce (or the sauce mix) with the wine and milk, as per page 249 (or according to manufacturer's instructions).

4. Add the flageolet beans, salmon, drained pasta, pepper and green beans, mixing together gently but thoroughly.

5. Stir in the cream and dill if using and season to taste.

GRAINS

Unless you are a strict vegetarian, the most common grain used by the average cook is rice. Others are wheat, corn, barley, millet, oats and rye. Grains provide valuable fibre, some minerals and have a low fat content.

Brown rice is now preferred by many for its nutty flavour and firm texture, compared to the softer, blander taste of white rice. Wild rice, although expensive, is also popular. It is not strictly a rice, being the grains from wild grasses, but is delicious and well worth keeping in stock.

Traditionally a risotto should be creamier than a pillau. Unless you use the special Italian risotto rice, which is sold at some supermarkets, you are unlikely to achieve any difference.

You can use just about anything in a risotto or pillau. Experiment with your own favourite combinations of meat, fish, vegetables and even fruit. Some of the following recipes include brown rice, but by substituting white rice the cooking time is halved: 30-40 minutes for brown and 10-20 minutes for white. Allow between 2-3 oz (50-75g) of rice per person.

LAMB PILAU   *Serves 4*

Lamb and coriander complement each other beautifully, resulting in a succulent and tasty supper dish.

Preparation time: 10 mins.   *Cooking time: 40 mins.*

2 tablsp cooking oil
1 onion, peeled and chopped
1 teasp coriander seeds
8 oz (225g) button mushrooms
12 oz (350g) leg or fillet lamb
Salt and pepper
2 tablsp sultanas

(continued overleaf)

12 oz (350g) brown rice (for white rice, see page 79)
1 stock cube, made up with 1¼ pt (650ml) water

1. Heat the oil in a large saucepan and add the onion.

2. Crush the coriander seeds with a rolling pin and add them to the pan together with the mushrooms.

3. Cut the lamb into bite-size pieces and add to the pan together with seasoning, sultanas and rice.

4. Fry for about 5 minutes to brown the meat.

5. Stir in the stock, bring to the boil and simmer with a lid on for about 40 minutes. Check during the last ten minutes and add more water if necessary.

PORK RISOTTO WITH CIDER   *Serves 4*

For economy, reduce the amount of meat and add more vegetables.

Preparation time: 10 mins.   *Cooking time: 40 mins.*

1 lb (450g) leg of pork or tenderloin
1 onion, peeled and chopped
1 cooking apple, peeled, cored and sliced
2 sticks celery, sliced
8 oz (225g) brown rice (for white rice, see page 79)
2 tablsp cooking oil
1 tablsp chopped fresh sage OR 1 teasp dried
2 teasp mustard powder
¾ pt (400ml) medium-sweet cider
1 stock cube, made up with ¼ pt (150ml) water
3 oz (75g) packet nuts and raisins
Salt and pepper

1. Cut the pork into bite-size pieces and put it in a large

saucepan together with the onion, apple, celery, rice and oil.

2. Fry over a high heat until the meat has browned on all sides.

3. Stir in all the remaining ingredients, bring to the boil and simmer gently for about 40 minutes with a lid on. Check during the last ten minutes and add a little water if necessary.

CHINESE EGG FRIED RICE   *Serves 4*

Serve on its own or with a tomato and cheese salad.

Preparation time: 10 mins.   *Cooking time: 20 mins.*

12 oz (350g) white long-grain rice
Salt
2 tablsp cooking oil
2 cloves garlic, peeled and finely chopped
4 spring onions, sliced
1 tablsp sesame seeds
1 red pepper, de-seeded and chopped
4 oz (100g) mushrooms, sliced
1 tablsp soy sauce
6 oz (175g) peeled prawns
Freshly ground black pepper
2 eggs, beaten

1. Cook the rice in boiling salted water until tender, about 10 minutes. Drain.

2. Heat the oil in a large frying pan and add the garlic, spring onions, sesame seeds, red pepper and mushrooms. Fry until the vegetables are tender, about 10 minutes.

3. Stir in the drained rice, soy sauce, prawns and black pepper and fry for a further few minutes, stirring well.

(continued overleaf)

4. Make a well in the centre of the rice and pour in the beaten egg. Fry over a high heat, stirring the egg well through the rice as it scrambles.

VEGETABLE RISOTTO   *Serves 4*

This mildly spiced risotto is ideal to serve with cold meat or kebabs. On its own as a vegetarian meal it could be accompanied by garlic bread or a cheese and tomato salad.

Preparation time: 12 mins.   *Cooking time: 40 mins.*

4 tablsp cooking oil
1 onion, peeled and chopped
2 leeks, washed and sliced
3 sticks celery, sliced
1 red pepper, de-seeded and sliced
4 oz (100g) mushrooms, sliced
Knob fresh ginger, grated
1 teasp garam masala
1 teasp turmeric
1 teasp chilli powder
2 teasp paprika
3 teasp yeast extract
8 oz (225g) brown rice (for white rice, see page 79)
Scant 1 pt (500ml) water
14 oz (397g) can chopped tomatoes

1. Heat the oil in a large saucepan and throw in all the prepared vegetables, ginger, spices, yeast extract and rice.

2. Fry for a few minutes, stirring well.

3. Pour in the water, bring to the boil and simmer, with the

lid on, for about 40 minutes until the rice is tender. Check during the last ten minutes and add a little water if necessary.

4. Stir in the tomatoes and adjust seasoning.

AUBERGINE AND BULGAR WHEAT SUPPER
Serves 4

Serve with a green salad and fresh crusty bread.

Preparation time: 15 mins.   *Cooking time: 18 mins.*

3 oz (75g) bulgar wheat
2 aubergines, diced
2 onions, peeled and roughly chopped
3 fl oz (75ml) cooking oil
14 oz (397g) can tomatoes, drained
Dark and Spicy Dressing (see next recipe)
Salt and pepper
Chopped parsley for garnish (optional)

1. Put the bulgar wheat in a bowl and pour on enough boiling water to cover. Leave to stand for 15 minutes then drain.

2. Meanwhile fry the aubergines and onions in the oil until tender, about 15 minutes.

3. Stir in the tomatoes, bulgar wheat and about 4 table-spoons Dark and Spicy Dressing. Season and garnish with chopped parsley if liked.

DARK AND SPICY DRESSING

A piquant flavour which makes a good dressing for bland foods such as bean salads.

Preparation time: 1 min.

5 fl oz (150ml) olive oil
2½ fl oz (75ml) raspberry vinegar OR red wine vinegar
Salt and pepper
½ teasp coriander
½ teasp cumin
Pinch cayenne
½ teasp mustard powder

Shake all the ingredients well together in a screw-top jar.

TUNA MEXICANA   *Serves 4*

This quick one-pan recipe makes a tasty supper dish and is similar to the type of ready-prepared meal on the market, but infinitely cheaper.

Preparation time: 8 mins.   *Cooking time: 15 mins.*

8 oz (225g) long-grain rice
1 onion, peeled and chopped
1 red pepper, de-seeded and sliced
2 tablsp tomato purée
2 teasp Mexican chilli seasoning
Salt and pepper
1 stock cube, made up with scant 1 pt (500ml) water
7 oz (200g) can sweetcorn, drained
8 oz (225g) can red kidney beans, drained
7 oz (200g) can tuna fish, drained and flaked
Juice 1 lemon

1. Put the rice, onion, red pepper, tomato purée, chilli seasoning, salt, pepper and stock into a saucepan.

2. Bring to the boil and simmer with a tight-fitting lid for about 15 minutes until the rice is tender.

3. Stir in the corn, beans, tuna fish and lemon juice and heat through for a couple of minutes. Serve with hot garlic bread.

BOMBAY PILAU   *Serves 4*

Another throw-it-all-in-the-pot recipe; everything except the fresh vegetables should be in stock! For added substance, meat-eaters could add some diced cooked ham, beef or chicken. The pilau is delicious served with Chick Pea Dhal (see page 87).

Preparation time: 12 mins.   *Cooking time: 20 mins*

4 tablsp cooking oil
2 teasp fenugreek seeds
2 teasp ground coriander
1 teasp ground cumin
1 teasp turmeric
½ teasp chilli powder
1 aubergine, diced
1 clove garlic, peeled and crushed
1 onion, peeled and chopped
4 oz (100g) mushrooms, sliced
knob fresh ginger, peeled and coarsely grated
1 green pepper, de-seeded and diced
Salt and pepper
8 oz (225g) Basmati rice
15 fl oz (400ml) water

1. Heat the oil in a saucepan and add the next 5 ingredients.

(continued overleaf)

2. Add the prepared vegetables to the spice mixture in the order given in the list of ingredients.

3. Add a generous shake of salt and pepper and cook gently for 10 minutes, stirring frequently.

4. Stir in the rice and cook for a couple of minutes.

5. Add the water, cover the pan and simmer for about 10 minutes until the rice is tender. (Check occasionally and add more water if the mixture is sticking.)

PULSES

Pulse is the word which encompasses peas, beans and lentils. These rather humble (and much maligned) objects have enjoyed a renaissance in recent years. The range of canned and dried peas and beans sold by ordinary supermarkets has increased enormously.

Pulses are a rich source of protein and fibre and are low in fat, but best of all, perhaps, they are cheap.

Dried peas and beans have to be soaked overnight. This helps them to swell so that cooking time is reduced. Soaking also helps remove some of the agents which cause indigestion and flatulence. They also take about one hour to cook. For this reason I recommend using the excellent canned varieties on the market.

Lentils do not need soaking; split red lentils are the most common type and although quick to cook – about 15 minutes – they have a soft texture and go mushy.

Green or brown (also known as Continental) lentils take longer to cook – about 45 minutes – but are preferred by many for their nutty flavour and ability to remain whole during cooking.

With the addition of flavourful herbs, spices and dressings, pulses can form the basis for all manner of interesting meals, both hot in casseroles or cold in salads.

CHICK PEA DHAL   *Serves 4*

Preparation time: 5 mins.   *Cooking time: 10 mins.*

15½ oz (440g) can chick peas
Knob ginger, peeled and coarsely grated
1 fresh chilli, chopped
1 clove garlic, peeled and crushed
Juice 1 lemon
Salt and pepper
1 teasp mustard seeds
1 teasp turmeric
1 teasp ground cumin
1 teasp ground coriander

1. Put the chick peas, with the liquor, into a small saucepan and add all the other ingredients.

2. Bring to the boil then simmer for about 10 minutes until the liquid has reduced and thickened. Mash the chick peas a little with the back of a spoon.

3. Serve the Dhal as a accompaniment to other dishes.

LENTIL AND POTATO SUPPER   *Serves 4*

This makes a tasty and substantial supper dish and can be served with a green salad tossed in a well-flavoured dressing.

Preparation time: 10 mins.   *Cooking time: 30 mins.*

4 oz (100g) smoked streaky bacon, cut into pieces
2 celery sticks, sliced
1 onion, peeled and chopped
1 lb (450g) potatoes, peeled and diced
1 tablsp cooking oil
8 oz (225g) red lentils

(continued overleaf)

14 oz (397g) can chopped tomatoes
1 tablsp Worcestershire sauce
1 stock cube, made up with 1 pt (500ml) water
Salt and pepper

1. Fry the bacon, celery, onion and potatoes in the oil for 10 minutes.

2. Stir in the lentils, tomatoes, Worcestershire sauce, stock and seasoning.

3. Bring to the boil and simmer gently for about 20 minutes until the lentils and vegetables are tender.

LENTIL MOUSSAKA   *Serves 4*

If liked, add some chopped salami or pepperoni at the same time as the tomatoes.

Preparation time: 10 mins.   *Cooking time: 25 mins.*

6 oz (175g) red lentils
1 onion, peeled and roughly chopped
Salt and pepper
2 tablsp yeast extract
1½ pt (800ml) water
1 aubergine, diced
4 tablsp cooking oil
1 egg, beaten
2 tablsp milk
3 oz (75g) mature Cheddar cheese, grated
2 oz (50g) hazelnuts
14 oz (397g) can chopped tomatoes

1. Pre-heat oven to 200°C (400°F) or Gas No 6.

2. Put the lentils, onion, seasoning, yeast extract and water in a saucepan. Bring to the boil and simmer for about 10 minutes until the lentils are tender.

3. Meanwhile fry the diced aubergine in the oil for about 10 minutes.

4. Mix the egg, milk and cheese together for the topping.

5. Drain the lentils, stir in the hazelnuts and tomatoes and pour the mixture into an ovenproof dish.

6. Top with the fried aubergine and pour on the cheese topping. Bake in oven for about 15 minutes.

CHEESE AND LENTIL LOAF   *Serves 4*

Cayenne pepper gives a kick to this supper dish. Add more or less, according to personal taste. Serve hot or cold with a mayonnaise-based dressing such as mustard sauce (see page 118). Mixed salad and garlic bread make ideal accompaniments.

Preparation time: 10 mins.   *Cooking time: 45 mins.*

6 oz (175g) red lentils
1 teasp salt
12 fl oz (350ml) water
4 oz (100g) mature Cheddar cheese, grated
1 onion, peeled and chopped
½ teasp cayenne pepper
Juice ½ lemon
1 egg, beaten
3 tablsp single cream
Freshly ground black pepper

1. Pre-heat oven to 190°C (375°F) or Gas No 5.

(continued overleaf)

2. Cook the lentils in the salt and water for about 15 minutes. The mixture should resemble a stiff purée.

3. Stir in the grated cheese, onion, cayenne, lemon juice, egg, cream and pepper and mix thoroughly.

4. Pour the mixture into a greased loaf tin and bake for about 45 minutes. Leave to rest for 10 minutes before turning out.

CHICK PEA AND ARTICHOKE GRATIN   *Serves 4*

Chick peas have a pleasant creamy texture and nutty flavour and blend well with artichokes in this crunchy topped supper dish.

Preparation time: 12 mins.   *Cooking time: 12 mins.*

14 oz (400g) can artichoke hearts
14 oz (400g) can chick peas
½ pt (300ml) onion sauce, made with ½ vegetable juice,
   ½ milk (see page 250) OR 1 packet (25g size) onion
   sauce mix made with vegetable juice and milk, as above
3 oz (75g) packet parsley & thyme stuffing mix
2 oz (50g) mature Cheddar cheese, grated

1. Pre-heat oven to 200°C (400°F) or Gas No 6.

2. Drain the artichoke hearts, reserving the juice.

3. Drain the chick peas and mix both vegetables together in a bowl.

4. Make the onion sauce using half artichoke juice and half milk, as per page 250 or following manufacturer's instructions.

5. Mix the vegetables and sauce well together and turn mixture into a shallow ovenproof dish.

6. Combine the stuffing mix and cheese and sprinkle on top. Bake in oven for about 12 minutes.

BEAN AND VEGETABLE HOT POT   *Serves 4-6*

This is a chuck-it-all-in-one-pot recipe and resembles something between a casserole and a hearty soup. In spite of the use of Indian spices, the dish is not 'hot', or highly flavoured. You can use any combination of beans and vegetables, it will always taste good. Serve with crusty bread and butter.

Preparation time: 10 mins.   *Cooking time: 20 mins.*

2 medium potatoes, peeled and cut into small dice
1 onion, peeled and chopped
2 celery sticks, sliced
1 clove garlic, peeled and finely chopped
14 oz (400g) can flageolet beans
14 oz (400g) can chick peas, drained
14 oz (397g) can chopped tomatoes
Salt and pepper
1 teasp ground coriander
1 teasp ground cumin
1 teasp chilli powder
2 oz (50g) bulgar wheat

1. Put all the prepared vegetables, beans, plus liquor, drained chick peas, tomatoes, seasoning, spices and bulgar wheat in a saucepan.

2. Bring to the boil, stirring well, then simmer for about 20 minutes until the potato is tender.

9   FISH

For an island nation which invented the famous 'fish and chips', the British are notoriously squeamish when it comes to trying out new varieties of fish.

Be adventurous! Some of the more unusual fish now offered by fishmongers and the larger supermarkets are well worth trying, if only for convenience. Fish cooks quickly so is a boon to the busy cook.

Although dozens of interesting and exotic dishes can be made by combining fish with other ingredients, often the simplest is the nicest.

Try frying a slice of tuna, swordfish or shark in a little olive oil and a clove of finely chopped garlic. Serve sprinkled with lemon or lime juice, ground black pepper and a few chopped fresh herbs. A mixture of parsley and dill is particularly good, but fennel, chervil, lemon verbena or basil are all suitable.

Either accompany with a crisp green salad, or promote a Mediterranean flavour by frying a mixture of finely diced aubergine, green pepper and tomatoes alongside the fish.

MONKFISH KEBABS

The firm meaty texture of monkfish is not unlike lobster and is excellent for kebabs. For economy, substitute halibut, or intersperse the monkfish with chunks of vegetables. Allow about 1 lb (450g) of fish to serve four people. Cut the fish into bite-size pieces, thread on skewers and grill for about 10 minutes, brushing frequently with one of the following marinades.

SPICY MARINADE

2 tablsp cooking oil
Juice 1 lemon
Salt and pepper
2 teasp coriander seeds, crushed
1 teasp paprika
1 teasp Tabasco sauce

Combine all the ingredients.

GARLIC BUTTER

2 oz (50g) butter
1 clove garlic, peeled and finely chopped
Squeeze lemon juice
1 tablsp chopped parsley

Combine all the ingredients and spread on the kebabs. As the butter melts under the grill, brush the liquid frequently over the fish.

CANTONESE MARINADE   (adds an exotic flavour to fish)

4 tablsp cooking oil
3 tablsp white wine
2 teasp soy sauce
1 clove garlic, peeled and finely chopped
1 teasp dry ginger

Combine all the ingredients well.

FISH PUFFS

These make a nice light supper dish and are usually popular with children. Serve with salad and plenty of tartare (see page 96) or tomato sauce.

Preparation time: 20 mins.   *Cooking time: 10 mins.*

8 oz (225g) white fish (cod, haddock or coley)
4 tablsp milk
Salt and freshly ground black pepper
1 oz (25g) margarine
1 oz (25g) flour
1 size 3 egg, beaten
Oil for frying

1. Put the fish, milk, salt and pepper in a small saucepan, bring to the boil and simmer for 5-10 minutes depending on thickness. Drain but reserve the liquid.

2. Melt the margarine in a saucepan, add the flour and stir for 1 minute over a low heat.

3. Gradually add the fish liquor (use 4 tablespoonfuls and make up with cold milk if necessary). Cook for a further couple of minutes, stirring all the time, until the mixture forms a thick ball leaving the sides of the pan clean.

4. Remove from the heat and beat in the beaten egg a little at a time.

5. Flake the fish and mix it thoroughly into the egg mixture. Leave to cool.

6. Heat a deep pan of oil and drop in teaspoons of the mixture.

7. Fry for about 8 minutes until the fish balls are crisp and golden. Drain on kitchen paper.

Note: The food should bubble very gently; if the oil is too hot the mixture will be burnt on the outside and raw inside.

FISH CAKES

Serves 4

Fish cakes are a good way of making a little fish go a long way and also encouraging children to eat fish when otherwise they may not be keen. By making your own you know exactly what has gone into them!

Preparation time: 20 mins.   *Cooking time: 20 mins.*

1 lb (450g) potatoes, peeled and cut into pieces
8 oz (225g) white fish (cod, haddock or coley)
Salt and freshly ground black pepper
1 tablsp freshly chopped parsley (optional)
Little finely grated lemon rind (optional)
1 size 3 egg, beaten
Breadcrumbs ⎤ **for coating**
Beaten egg ⎦

1. Cook the potatoes in boiling, salted water for about 15-20 minutes until tender. Drain and mash.

2. Meanwhile, put the fish in enough salted water to barely cover it and cook over a low heat for about 8-10 minutes depending on thickness. Then drain the fish, peel off the skin and pull out any bones.

3. Flake the fish into a bowl and mix in the mashed potato, salt, pepper, parsley and lemon rind (if using) and the beaten egg. Bind well and allow to cool.

4. Turn the mixture on to a floured board and form into 8 patties.

5. Brush both sides with beaten egg and then dip into breadcrumbs.

6. Fry the fish cakes in oil (use enough to come half way up the cakes) for about 8-10 minutes on each side until crisp and golden. Drain on kitchen paper.

Tip: As an alternative to flavouring the fish cakes with lemon rind, try 2 teaspoons of Worcestershire sauce.

95

CHIP SHOP FISH SUPPER

Serves 4

A firm family favourite when served with chips and peas. Use cod, haddock, coley or whiting.

Preparation time: 10 mins.   *Cooking time: 10 mins.*

¼ pt (150ml) fritter batter (see page 237)
2 tablsp flour
Salt and freshly ground black pepper
4 fillets white fish

1. Make the batter as per page 237.

2. Mix the flour, salt and pepper together and coat the fish with the seasoned flour.

3. Dip the fish in the batter and deep fry for about 10 minutes, according to thickness. Drain on kitchen paper.

Tip: I always feel there is something missing if I eat fried fish without **tartare sauce**. If you feel adventurous, why not make your own? It's much cheaper, and really very simple: stir a chopped pickled gherkin, a few chopped chives or parsley and a teaspoon of gherkin vinegar into some mayonnaise. Jars of pickled gherkins will keep for weeks.

FISH PROVENÇAL

Serves 4

A recipe with Greek origins. The lemon, garlic and tomatoes combine to make a tasty sauce in which the fish cooks.

Preparation time: 10 mins.   *Cooking time: 25 mins.*

1 onion, peeled and chopped
1 clove garlic, peeled and finely chopped
½ tablsp cooking oil
4 tomatoes, cut into pieces
Grated rind and juice of 1 lemon

Salt and pepper
1 lb (450g) white fish (cod, haddock, coley, etc.)

1. Pre-heat the oven to 190°C (375°F) or Gas No 5.

2. Fry the onion and garlic in the oil until tender.

3. Add the tomatoes, lemon rind and juice and seasoning.

4. Wash and pat dry the fillets of fish and put them in a shallow ovenproof dish. Pour over the tomato mixture and bake in oven for about 15 minutes, depending on the thickness of the fish.

LIME AND CHILLI SOUSED MACKEREL   *Serves 4*

The combination of tangy lime and hot chilli counteracts the richness of the mackerel well. The fish can be served hot, although personally I prefer it cold with salad and crusty bread and butter.

Preparation time: 8 mins.   *Cooking time: 10 mins.*
Marinading time: 30 mins. (if possible)

4 mackerel
Grated rind and juice of 1 lime
½ tablsp hot pepper OR chilli sauce
1 teasp soft brown sugar
Salt and pepper
2 tablsp chopped parsley for garnish (optional)

1. Although it is not difficult to bone mackerel, for quickness I usually ask my fishmonger to do the job. Using a sharp knife, score the mackerel at ½" (1cm) intervals. Place the fish close together in a shallow dish.

2. Combine the grated rind and lime juice, pepper or chilli sauce, sugar and seasoning. Pour over the mackerel,

(continued overleaf)

brushing it well into the cuts. If possible leave to marinade for 30 minutes.

3. Place the mackerel in a grill pan and grill under a medium heat for about 10 minutes. There is no need to turn the fish, but brush it frequently with the marinade.

4. If liked, the skin can be peeled off before serving. Garnish with chopped parsley.

Tip: Herrings could also be treated in this way.

SMOKED MACKEREL PÂTÉ
Serves 4 as a main course or 6 as a starter

With a food processor the preparation of this tasty pâté takes literally seconds. However even by hand it only takes 10 minutes. Although not essential the cayenne pepper gives a 'bite' to the pâté without making it at all 'hot'. Serve with plenty of fresh brown bread for a perfect light lunch or supper.

Preparation time: 10 mins.   *Cooking time: none*

8 oz (225g) smoked mackerel (about 2 fillets)
4 oz (110g) carton cream cheese
Juice 1 lemon
½ level teasp cayenne pepper (optional)
Salt and freshly ground black pepper

1. Peel the skin off the mackerel, remove any bones and then mash the flesh in a bowl.

2. In a separate bowl soften the cheese with a wooden spoon and then gradually mix in the lemon juice alternately with the mackerel.

3. Stir in the cayenne, a little salt and plenty of black pepper. Mix well, press into a shallow dish and chill before serving.

GRILLED MACKEREL

Allow one small to medium sized fish per person. Mackerel is particularly good served cold and goes well with spicy or tangy flavours. Simply trickle the cooked fish with lemon or lime juice, plenty of freshly ground black pepper and serve with salad and crusty bread.

Preparation time: 5 mins.   *Cooking time: 10 mins.*

Small to medium sized mackerel, boned
Oil
Salt and freshly ground black pepper

1. Pre-heat grill to medium.

2. Make 3 or 4 cuts in the mackerel, season the inside of the fish with salt and pepper and brush the outside with oil.

3. Grill for about 5 minutes on each side. If liked the skin can be removed before serving.

Tip: Herrings can be cooked in the same way.

BAKED MACKEREL WITH VEGETABLES *Serves 4*

Mackerel fillets cooked on a bed of diced vegetables make a good light supper dish. Serve with plenty of fresh crusty bread.

Preparation time: 15 mins.   *Cooking time: 25-30 mins.*

2 tablsp oil
1 onion, peeled and chopped
1 red pepper, diced
4 oz (100g) button mushrooms, sliced
1 lb (450g) courgettes, diced
4 small mackerel OR 2 large, boned
Salt and freshly ground black pepper

1. Pre-heat the oven to 180°C (350°F) or Gas No 4.

(continued overleaf)

2. Heat the oil and gently fry the onion, pepper, mushrooms and courgettes for 5 minutes. Drain and place in a shallow ovenproof dish.

3. Flatten out the mackerel and, if large, cut into two lengthways.

4. Season with salt and pepper, place on top of the vegetables. Cover with foil and bake for 25-30 minutes.

MUSTARD AND YOGHURT-GLAZED PLAICE
Serves 4

My husband, not the greatest of fish lovers, said how much he enjoyed this recipe!

Preparation time: 4 mins.   *Cooking time: 8 mins.*

4 fillets plaice
Salt and pepper
Splash white wine OR milk
3 tablsp natural yoghurt
3 teasp French mustard
Grated Parmesan cheese

1. Pre-heat oven to 200°C (400°F) or Gas No 6.

2. Sprinkle the fillets with salt and pepper and place them in a shallow ovenproof dish. Pour in a splash of wine or milk just to cover the bottom of the dish.

3. Mix the yoghurt and mustard together and spread on the fish. Sprinkle with Parmesan cheese.

4. Bake in oven for about 8 minutes depending on thickness of the fish. Serve with sauté potatoes and green vegetables.

SOLE VERONIQUE   *Serves 4*

This is a classic dish traditionally made with what is known in the trade as allemande sauce. This is made with lemon juice, egg yolks, wine and cream. Here is my quick, and just as tasty, version using a packet sauce mix. For a special occasion you could add a few prawns with the grapes and serve in individual scallop shells as a starter.

Preparation time: 10 mins.   *Cooking time: 20 mins.*

4 fillets sole (plaice could be substituted)
4 oz (100g) white grapes
Salt and pepper
¼ pt (150ml) white wine
Packet (standard/25g size) Hollandaise sauce mix
  (makes ½ pt/300ml)
Milk

1. Pre-heat oven to 190°C (375°F) or Gas No 5.

2. Lay the fillets skin-side up on a board.

3. Halve the grapes and remove pips. (By rights the grapes should also be peeled but this is not essential.) Divide the grapes between the fillets and season well with salt and pepper.

4. Fold the fillets lengthwise into three and place them in a shallow ovenproof dish.

5. Pour on the wine, cover with foil and cook in oven for about 15 minutes, depending on thickness of the fish.

6. Drain the fish and keep warm. Make up the sauce mix according to manufacturer's instructions using the fish liquor, and milk if necessary, to the required amount.

7. Pour the sauce over the fish and garnish with chopped parsley if liked.

PRAWN AND CASHEW STIR-FRY *Serves 4*

This is a good recipe for making a few prawns go a long way. Serve with thin Chinese-style noodles.

Preparation time: 10 mins.   *Cooking time: 15 mins.*

1 onion, peeled and chopped
4 courgettes, sliced
4 oz (100g) mushrooms, sliced
2 tablsp cooking oil
8 oz (225g) beansprouts
Juice 1 lemon
1 tablsp soy sauce
3 oz (75g) cashew nuts
8 oz (225g) peeled prawns

1. Fry the onion, courgettes and mushrooms in the oil for about 10 minutes.

2. Stir in the beansprouts, lemon juice, soy sauce, cashew nuts and prawns and cook for a further 5 minutes.

PRAWN CREOLE *Serves 3-4*

Be warned – this is a real hot one! It's a throw-it-all-in-a-saucepan recipe and excellent served with garlic bread and green salad.

Preparation time: 10 mins.   *Cooking time: 20 mins.*

Packet (5 oz/120g size) curry-flavoured rice
4 fresh chillies, chopped
8 oz (225g) broccoli, cut into small florets
14 oz (397g) can chopped tomatoes
Juice 1 lemon
8 oz (225g) peeled prawns
5 fl oz (150ml) carton soured cream (optional)

1. Put the rice in a saucepan with water according to manu-facturer's instructions. (Follow exactly so there will be little or no liquid at the end.)

2. Simmer gently for 10 minutes then add the chillies and broccoli and complete the cooking time.

3. Stir in the tomatoes, lemon juice, prawns and soured cream, if using. Heat for a further couple of minutes.

COQUILLES ST JACQUES
Serves 4 as a starter or 2 as a main course

Delicately flavoured and firm-textured scallops are unfor-tunately expensive. Although in season from October to March they are now widely available frozen. This recipe is perhaps too costly for family meals, but if you are enter-taining, scallops make a delicious main course or starter. To make the scallops go further, combine with other firm fleshed white fish and a few prawns to make a wonderful seafood medley.

Preparation time: 5 mins.   *Cooking time: 10 mins.*

**Handful dried sliced mushrooms (use fresh if
    you prefer)**
8 scallops
¼ pt (150ml) white wine
Shake salt
Freshly ground black pepper
Piece raw onion, peeled
1 tablsp flour
1 tablsp butter or margarine
2-3 tablsp single cream
Grated Parmesan cheese

(continued overleaf)

COQUILLES ST JACQUES *continued*

1. Put the dried mushrooms in a cup and pour on boiling water.

2. Put the scallops, wine, salt, pepper and onion in a small pan. Bring to the boil and simmer for about 5 minutes until the scallops are tender.

3. Meanwhile blend the flour and butter or margarine in a small bowl.

4. Lift out the scallops with a slotted spoon and place them in a warm serving dish or individual scallop shells. Drain the mushrooms and scatter over.

5. Add the blended flour and butter to the scallop liquor and stir over a medium heat until thickened. Stir in the cream and adjust seasoning.

6. Pour the sauce over the scallops, sprinkle liberally with grated Parmesan cheese and brown under a hot grill for a couple of minutes.

POACHED FRESH SALMON

Largely due to fish farming, salmon is one of the few foods which has dropped in price in recent years. It is now almost half the cost of fillet steak and, according to the experts, is infinitely healthier. Research shows that the fatty acids, known as omega 3s, which are concentrated in cold water fish, help protect against a long string of diseases including blood clotting and strokes.

Salmon is usually sold in middle steaks or cutlets, or tail end fillets. Allow about 4 oz (100g) per person.

Preparation time: 5 mins.　　　　　*Cooking time: 10 mins.*

Water
Piece raw peeled onion

6 peppercorns
Bay leaf
1 teasp salt
Juice 1 lemon

1. Place the salmon in a saucepan with enough water to barely cover it. (A mixture of water and white wine can be used if preferred.)

2. Add the remainder of the ingredients, bring to the boil then simmer gently for about 10 minutes. Unless serving hot, allow the salmon to cool in the liquor. Peel off the skin and discard.

The delicate flavour of this unique fish needs little or no embellishment making it an ideal choice for the busy cook. The exception perhaps is French mayonnaise or an alternative good quality side-of-plate dressing. Here are two of my favourites.

WATERCRESS MOUSSELINE   *Serves 4*

Preparation time: 5 mins.

1 bunch watercress
3 tablsp double cream
3 tablsp French-style mayonnaise
Salt and black pepper
Juice ½ lemon

1. Cut the stalks off the watercress and chop the leaves.

2. Mix the leaves, cream, mayonnaise, seasoning and lemon juice well together.

RASPBERRY AND CRANBERRY SAUCE   *Serves 4*

Preparation time: 2 mins.   *Cooking time: 5 mins.*

4 oz (100g) raspberries
2 tablsp cranberry jelly
Juice ½ lemon

> Put the three ingredients into a small pan and heat gently
> until the cranberry jelly melts. Boil for about 5 minutes
> until the liquid has reduced and thickened. Mash the
> raspberries lightly and leave in the fridge until cold.

SALMON KEDGEREE   *Serves 3-4*

This delicately flavoured and delicious kedgeree is ideal for a
light supper. Its economical use of salmon makes it light on
the pocket too. For quickness you can use canned salmon but
surprisingly there is little difference in cost. Fresh dill is by
far superior to dried in this recipe but if you can't get it, use a
bunch of chopped watercress leaves instead. Serve with
crusty bread and a tomato salad.

Preparation time: 8 mins.   *Cooking time: 35 mins.*

8 oz (225g) wild rice (see page 79)
½ teasp salt
½ cucumber, peeled and diced
Juice 1 lemon
1 tablsp chopped fresh dill
Freshly ground black pepper
8 oz (225g) cold cooked salmon OR 1 (7½ oz/213g) can,
** drained and flaked**
Onion in wafer thin slices for garnish (optional)

1. Cook the rice according to the manufacturer's instructions, using the stated amount of water.

2. Add salt, cucumber, lemon juice, dill, pepper and salmon.
   Serve warm or cold and garnish with onion if liked.

TUNA AND BROCCOLI MORNAY
Serves 3-4

This tasty dish could be made with salmon but tuna is cheaper. Serve with savoury rice.

Preparation time: 10 mins.   *Cooking time: 30 mins.*

1 lb (450g) broccoli, fresh or frozen
Packet Hollandaise sauce mix
½ pt (300ml) milk
Large (14 oz/397g) can tuna fish OR 15½ oz (440g)
  salmon, drained and flaked
2 oz (50g) mature Cheddar cheese, grated

1. Pre-heat oven to 190°C (375°F) or Gas No 5.

2. Break the broccoli into florets and cook in boiling salted water for 8-10 minutes until just tender. Drain.

3. Meanwhile make up the Hollandaise sauce with the milk according to manufacturer's instructions.

4. Put the drained broccoli and the flaked tuna or salmon into a shallow ovenproof dish and pour over the sauce.

5. Top with grated cheese and bake in oven for about 20 minutes until brown and bubbly.

SMOKED HADDOCK FRICASSEE
Serves 4

The combination of orange and Worcestershire sauce creates a nice flavour which tempts children if they're not too keen on fish.

Preparation time: 8 mins.   *Cooking time: 10 mins.*

12 oz (350g) smoked haddock
¼ pt (150ml) milk
Salt and pepper
Handful frozen peas

(continued overleaf)

SMOKED HADDOCK FRICASSEE continued

Small (11 oz/312g) can mandarin oranges
1 tablsp Worcestershire sauce
Packet (standard/17g size) white sauce mix (makes ½ pint)
7 oz (200g) can sweetcorn, drained

1. Poach the haddock in the milk and seasoning for about 6 minutes until the fish flakes easily.

2. Put the peas in a cup and pour on boiling water.

3. Blend 3 tablespoons of mandarin juice and the Worcestershire sauce with the sauce mix in a small pan.

4. Drain the fish, reserving the liquor. Remove skin and any bones and flake the flesh into a bowl.

5. Add the fish liquor to the sauce mix, bring to the boil and stir until thickened.

6. Mix the fish, sauce, drained peas, oranges and sweetcorn together and sprinkle with chopped parsley if liked. Serve with savoury rice.

SARDINES EN PAPILLOTTE   *Serves 4*

Sardines and trout are particularly good cooked in the French way, which literally means fish cooked in paper. Use grease-proof or foil and there isn't even any washing up! Supermarket fish departments or fishmongers will prepare the fish for you. Personal preference will dictate whether or not you leave on the heads.

Preparation time: 5 mins.   *Cooking time: 20 mins.*

8-12 fresh sardines
Salt and pepper
Juice 1 lemon
Roughly chopped herbs – parsley, dill, fennel or chives
1 courgette, sliced OR thick slices cucumber
2 tomatoes, sliced

108

1. Pre-heat oven to 190°C (375°F) or Gas No 5.

2. Brush four squares of greaseproof or foil with oil and put 2-3 washed sardines on each.

3. Sprinkle with salt and pepper, lemon juice and chopped herbs. Lay the slices of courgette, or cucumber, and tomato on top and season again.

4. Fold the paper or foil around the sardines into individual parcels and bake in the oven for about 20 minutes until the sardines and vegetables are tender. Serve with salad and savoury rice.

HADDOCK IN MUSHROOM SAUCE   *Serves 4*

Nothing could be quicker or easier to prepare. The mushroom soup forms a tasty coating-sauce and most varieties of white fish are suitable. For an even quicker version, omit the onion and heat a can of flaked tuna fish in the soup. Serve with savoury rice or matchstick fried potatoes and peas or tomatoes.

Preparation time: 5 mins.   *Cooking time: 25 mins.*

1 onion, peeled and chopped
6 oz (175g) mushrooms, sliced
4 fillets haddock
10.4 oz (295g) can condensed mushroom soup
3 tablsp milk
Chopped parsley for garnish (optional)

1. Pre-heat oven to 190°C (375°F) or Gas No 5.

2. Put the onion and mushrooms in a shallow ovenproof dish and lay the fish on top.

3. Pour on the soup and milk and give the dish a good shake to mix the liquids.

(continued overleaf)

4. Cover with foil and cook for about 25 minutes until the fish and vegetables are tender. (Halfway through cooking, give the dish another shake and remove the foil for the last 5 minutes.)

5. If liked, garnish with chopped parsley.

HADDOCK AND PRAWN CROISSANTS   *Serves 4*

Prawns add a touch of luxury to this recipe but make a more economical version by substituting a few cooked peas and/or some drained sweetcorn.

Preparation time: 5 mins.   *Cooking time: 15 mins.*

12 oz (350g) haddock fillets
½ pt (300ml) milk
Salt and pepper
4 croissants
Packet Hollandaise sauce mix
4 oz (100g) peeled prawns

1. Put the fish, milk and seasoning in a saucepan, bring to the boil and simmer gently for about 10 minutes until the fish is tender.

2. Slice the croissants in two horizontally but do not separate. Place on a baking tray and heat in a warm oven for 5 minutes.

3. Drain the fish, reserving the liquor. Remove skin if liked and roughly flake the flesh.

4. Make up the sauce mix, according to manufacturer's instructions, using the fish liquor.

5. Stir in fish and prawns.

6. Place each bottom half croissant on a plate, spoon on some fish mixture and top with the other half croissant.

7. Serve with a selection of vegetables cooked until just tender. Green beans, carrots and leeks are a good choice.

SEAFOOD VOL-AU-VENTS

The preparation for this dish can be done while the vol-au-vents are cooking, thus saving further time. If possible, use cooked fresh mussels which are usually available from fish departments of large supermarkets. If not, buy the mussels bottled in brine.

Preparation time: 10 mins.   *Cooking time: 12 mins.*

4 king-size frozen vol-au-vents
½ pt (300ml) white sauce (see page 249) or use 1 packet
  (17g size) white sauce mix
2 oz (50g) peeled prawns
2 oz (50g) cooked fresh mussels
7 oz (200g) can tuna fish, drained and flaked
7 oz (200g) can sweetcorn, drained
Swig sherry
Ground black pepper

1. Pre-heat oven to 220°C (425°F) or Gas No 7. Cook the vol-au-vents in the oven for about 12 minutes until well risen and lightly brown.

2. Meanwhile make up the white sauce as per page 249 or according to manufacturer's instructions with ½ pt (300ml) milk.

3. Stir in the prawns, mussels, tuna fish, corn, sherry and pepper. Mix well.

4. Remove the lids from the vol-au-vents and pull out and discard uncooked pastry.

5. Fill the vol-au-vents with the fish mixture, pop on the lids and heat in the oven for 3 minutes.

6. Serve with salad and some sliced chicory tossed in vinaigrette dressing.

111

SQUID STIR-FRY

Serves 4

A friend's husband kindly donated this recipe. (She said it was the only meal he ever cooked!) Squid is usually cut into rings but this method is more attractive and nicer to eat. The fish combines well with lightly cooked vegetables into a meal which is full of texture and flavour.

Preparation time: 15 mins.   *Cooking time: 10 mins.*

1½ lb (700g) small squid
2 tablsp cooking oil
2 tablsp soy sauce
2 cloves garlic, peeled and crushed
½ teasp chilli powder
8 oz (225g) broccoli, cut into small florets
4 oz (100g) mushrooms, sliced
1 carrot, grated

1. Cut off the tentacles below the ink sac. Split the squid down the side and flatten out. Scrape out innards and ink sac. Skin. You should be left with flat fillets.

2. With a sharp knife lightly score the fillets diagonally in both directions. Cut each squid into about four pieces. Wash and dry thoroughly.

3. Heat the oil, soy sauce, garlic and chilli powder in a wok or large frying pan.

4. Add the squid and the tentacles to the hot liquid and stir over a fairly high heat for 5 minutes.

5. Stir in the broccoli, mushrooms and carrot and continue stir-frying for a further 5 minutes.

6. Serve with rice.

10 MEAT

KEBABS

Kebabs make a quick meal and are especially delicious when marinaded in a tasty or spicy mixture before cooking. If you can spare 10 minutes the previous evening to prepare the marinade, all you have to do the following night is thread the meat on the skewers and throw them under the grill!

If energy and time are short, just rub the kebabs with a cut clove of garlic, trickle with lemon juice and season. Choose a selection of meat from the following:

Leg or fillet of lamb
Pork tenderloin
Rump or fillet steak
Boneless and skinless chicken portions
King prawns
Pieces of good butcher's sausage or Cumberland sausage
Liver, kidneys, bacon rolls

Allow about 4-6 oz (100-175g) meat per person and cut it

113

into bite-size pieces before marinading. Good, and therefore expensive, cuts of meat must be used for grilling but it can be 'stretched' with the addition of certain vegetables:

Chunks of red, green and yellow peppers
Pieces of marrow
Quarters of par-boiled onion
Chunks of aubergine
Courgettes, cut into three or four pieces
Small whole tomatoes
Button mushrooms

Use long metal or wooden skewers and cook under a medium grill, turning occasionally and brushing frequently with the marinade, or a little oil.

Kebabs are especially good served with wild rice and a salad tossed in a vinaigrette dressing.

MEDITERRANEAN MARINADE
(good with pork and lamb)

4 tablsp cooking oil
4 tablsp sherry
1 clove garlic, peeled and chopped
2 tablsp chopped fresh parsley
1 tablsp chopped fresh oregano or 1 teasp dried
Salt and pepper

Combine all the ingredients and marinade the meat overnight if possible.

LAMB OR CHICKEN TIKKA

Serves 4

This marinade has a thick consistency so doesn't really need to be left overnight.

Preparation time: 10 mins.   *Cooking time: 15 mins.*

1 lb (450g) leg or fillet of lamb
1 small onion, peeled and finely chopped
1 clove garlic, peeled and finely chopped
Juice 1 lemon
1 tablsp cooking oil
2 tablsp tomato purée
2 teasp ground coriander
1 teasp turmeric
1 teasp chilli powder
½ tablsp hot pepper or chilli sauce (optional)

1. Cut the lamb into bite-size pieces. (Chicken can be used if preferred.)

2. Mix the remaining ingredients together and stir in the meat.

3. Thread the meat on skewers, spoon over the remaining marinade and cook under a medium grill for about 15 minutes, turning occasionally.

SATAY KEBABS
(good with any of the meat listed on page 113)

Juice 1 lemon
1 clove garlic, peeled and chopped
1 tablsp chopped fresh mixed herbs OR 1 teasp dried
3 tablsp crunchy peanut butter
½ stock cube made with ¼ pt (150ml) water
1 onion, peeled and finely chopped

(continued overleaf)

1. Marinade the meat in the lemon juice, garlic and mixed herbs and leave overnight.

2. The next evening blend the peanut butter with the stock, onion and a little of the lemon marinade to give a coating consistency.

3. Thread the meat on skewers and spoon over the peanut mixture.

4. Cook under a gentle grill, turning occasionally and spooning on more of the peanut mixture.

CHINESE MARINADE
(good with all the meat listed on page 113)

2 tablsp soy sauce
1 tablsp cooking oil
Juice ½ lemon
1 teasp soft brown sugar
1 clove garlic, peeled and chopped
Knob fresh ginger, peeled and grated OR ½ teasp
  ground ginger

Combine all the ingredients well and marinade meat for several hours if possible.

MARYLAND KEBABS   *Serves 4*

Preparation time: 15 mins.   *Cooking time: 20 mins.*

6-8 boneless and skinless chicken thighs
1 tablsp soft brown sugar
1 tablsp Worcestershire sauce
Juice 1 lemon

4 rashers smoked streaky bacon
2 bananas

1. Cut each chicken thigh into four pieces.

2. Blend the sugar, Worcestershire sauce and lemon juice in a small bowl and stir in the chicken. Leave to marinade overnight.

3. The next evening cut the bacon rashers in two and the bananas into four pieces.

4. Wrap a piece of bacon around each piece of banana.

5. Thread the chicken and the bacon-wrapped bananas on skewers, brush well with the marinade and grill gently for about 10 minutes on each side.

SHEEK KEBABS   *Serves 4*

Preparation time: 15 mins.   *Cooking time: 15 mins.*

1 lb (450g) best minced beef
3 cloves garlic, peeled and finely chopped
Knob fresh ginger, peeled and grated
2 fresh chillies, finely chopped, OR 1 teasp dried crushed
  chillies
2 teasp ground coriander
1 tablsp curry paste or powder
1 egg, beaten

1. Mix all the ingredients together, using your hand if necessary to bind well.

2. With floured hands form the mixture into sausage shapes about 3" (7.5cm) long and thread two or three on each skewer.

3. Brush with oil and grill gently for about 15 minutes, turning occasionally. Serve hot or cold with Mustard Sauce (page 118).

117

SAUSAGE HERB AND GARLIC KEBABS *Serves 4*

This mixture can either be made into kebabs and served as a main course, or formed into balls (makes 40) and fried. These can be speared on cocktail sticks and handed round as 'nibbles' for bonfire night celebrations, Christmas and New Year get-togethers, or indeed any party occasion.

Preparation time: 15 mins.   *Cooking time: 15 mins.*

1 lb (450g) pork sausagemeat
4 oz (100g) packet herb and garlic stuffing mix
1 egg, beaten

1. Mix all the ingredients well together, using your hand if necessary.

2. Flour your hands and, if making kebabs, form the mixture into sausage shapes. If making party 'nibbles' roll the mixture into small balls.

3. Thread the kebabs on metal or wooden skewers and grill for about 15 minutes turning frequently. Fry the balls in hot oil for about 10 minutes and drain on kitchen paper. Serve with . . .

MUSTARD SAUCE

Preparation time: 8 mins.

6 tablsp mayonnaise
2 teasp English mustard
1 teasp lemon juice
1 teasp tomato ketchup
2 teasp Worcestershire sauce

Combine all the ingredients into a smooth cream.

PORK KEBABS WITH APRICOTS AND PINEAPPLE

Serves 4

Fruit goes particularly well with pork because it counteracts the rich meat.

Preparation time: 10 mins.   *Cooking time: 20-25 mins.*

1 lb (450g) pork tenderloin
8 dried apricots
8 oz (225g) can pineapple chunks
1 tablsp cooking oil
1 tablsp soy sauce
Knob fresh ginger, peeled and grated

1.   Cut pork into bite-size pieces.

2.   Put pork, apricots, pineapple and juice, oil, soy sauce and ginger into a bowl. Stir well and leave to marinade overnight.

3.   Thread meat and fruit alternately on skewers, brush with marinade and cook under a medium grill, turning occasionally, for 20-25 minutes.

CHICKEN LIME KEBABS

Serves 4

A delicious sweet and sour marinade.

Preparation time: 6 mins.   *Cooking time: 15 mins.*

8 boneless and skinless chicken thighs
1 tablsp tomato purée
Juice 1 lime
1 tablsp cooking oil
½ tablsp Worcestershire sauce

(continued overleaf)

2 tablsp lime marmalade
1 clove garlic, peeled and chopped

1. Cut each chicken thigh into four.

2. Blend the remaining ingredients well together and marinade the chicken overnight.

3. Thread the chicken on skewers, brush with the marinade and grill for about 15 minutes, turning occasionally.

LIVER AND BACON KEBABS *Serves 4*

The combination of liver and bacon is a traditional favourite. Try this tasty way of cooking for a change.

Preparation time: 8 mins.   *Cooking time: 10 mins.*

1 lb (450g) lamb's liver
6 oz (175g) smoked streaky bacon
4 oz (100g) button mushrooms
Juice 1 lemon
Salt and ground black pepper
Cooking oil

1. Cut the liver into ½" (1cm) pieces.

2. Cut the rashers of bacon into two and roll up each piece.

3. Thread the liver, bacon rolls and mushrooms alternately on skewers and sprinkle with lemon juice, salt and pepper.

4. Brush with oil and cook under a medium grill for about 10 minutes, turning once.

5. Serve with savoury rice and salad.

DEVILLED KIDNEY KEBABS   *Serves 4*

Kidneys are tender if cooked quickly which makes them ideal
for the busy cook. This spicy way of serving should appeal to
those members of the family who perhaps are not usually
keen on kidneys.

Preparation time: 8 mins.   *Cooking time: 10 mins.*

10-12 lamb's kidneys
1 teasp salt
½ teasp cayenne pepper
2 teasp mustard powder
2 teasp curry powder

1. Split the kidneys without actually dividing them. Using
    scissors, remove the white core and as many tubes as
    possible.

2. Make several slashes in the kidneys with a sharp knife.

3. Mix the salt, cayenne, mustard and curry powder
    together and rub into the kidneys.

4. Thread on skewers, brush with oil and cook under
    medium grill for about 5 minutes each side.

5. Serve with croûtons of fried bread and a tomato and
    chicory salad trickled with vinaigrette dressing.

STIR-FRIES

Stir-fry dishes offer unlimited scope for quick and tasty
meals. They are made, as the name implies, by stirring and
frying and are great for using up bits and pieces. That chunk
of green pepper, for example, which has been lying in the
fridge for days, the odd banana which no-one is willing to eat,
or the half used can of pineapple.

Pre-packaged and frozen stir-fry vegetables are now available from most supermarkets. They usually contain a combination of beansprouts, courgettes, onion, peppers, sweetcorn, mushrooms and water chestnuts. For quickness these are well worth using, but by preparing your own vegetables you can choose particular family favourites. Of the recipes listed here, one includes a pre-packaged mixture and five give ideas for home prepared veg.

Apart from the varieties already mentioned, most vegetables are suitable, including aubergine, cabbage, carrots, marrow, leeks, tomatoes, broccoli and sliced green beans.

By increasing or decreasing the meat content, stir-fry meals can be as expensive or as economical as you wish to make them. Meat quantities in the following recipes are given only as a suggestion.

Allow 1 lb-1¼ lb (450g-575g) of mixed vegetables if the dish contains meat, but about 2 lb (900g) if using vegetables only. (See also chapters on Fish and Vegetarian Meals.) Soya products like tofu can be stir-fried and substituted for meat or fish if liked.

Stir-fry meals are traditionally cooked in a Chinese wok, but a large frying pan will do. If possible, use sesame seed oil as it imparts an authentic seasoning and flavour.

CARIBBEAN STIR-FRY   *Serves 4*

The addition of mango and banana conveys an exotic flavour to this quickly made chicken dish.

Preparation time: 10 mins.   *Cooking time: 15 mins.*

10-12 oz (275g-350g) boneless and skinless chicken
Salt and pepper
2 tablsp sesame seed oil
1 onion, peeled and chopped
1 red pepper, de-seeded and sliced
2 courgettes, sliced

122

2 tablsp soy sauce
1 mango, peeled and sliced
1 banana, peeled and sliced
10 oz (275g) carton beansprouts
1 tablsp flaked almonds (optional)

1. Thinly slice the chicken and season with salt and pepper.

2. Fry quickly in the hot oil until sealed on both sides.

3. Add the onion, pepper, courgettes and soy sauce and stir-fry for about 10 minutes.

4. Add the mango, banana and beansprouts and fry for a further 5 minutes.

5. Serve sprinkled with flaked almonds if liked.

INDIAN STIR-FRY
Serves 4

Use boneless and skinless chicken or pork tenderloin in this subtly spiced recipe. Add a little chilli powder if you prefer a distinct 'kick'. Serve with rice.

Preparation time: 10 mins.　　　　*Cooking time: 15 mins.*

10-12 oz (275g-350g) pork or chicken
3 tablsp sesame seed oil
1 tablsp curry paste
4 oz (100g) mushrooms, sliced
1 aubergine, diced
1 onion, peeled and chopped
4 tomatoes, cut into pieces
2 tablsp sultanas
Desiccated coconut for garnish (optional)

1. Slice the pork or chicken.

(continued overleaf)

2. Heat the oil and curry paste and fry the meat quickly until sealed.

3. Add the vegetables and sultanas and stir-fry for about 15 minutes. (Aubergines absorb lots of oil so add a little more if the mixture looks too dry.) Serve sprinkled with coconut if liked.

CHINESE STIR-FRY   *Serves 4*

This recipe uses ready-prepared stir-fry vegetables which cuts down preparation time.

Preparation time: 5 mins.   *Cooking time: 15 mins.*

10-12 oz (275g-350g) pork or chicken
Salt and pepper
2 tablsp sesame seed oil
1 onion, peeled and chopped
1 tablsp soy sauce
8 oz (225g) can pineapple pieces
1 lb (450g) pack stir-fry vegetables

1. Slice the pork or chicken and season.

2. Fry the meat quickly in the hot oil until sealed on both sides.

3. Add the onion and soy sauce and stir-fry for about 10 minutes, until the meat is tender.

4. Add the pineapple pieces with a couple of tablespoons of juice, and the vegetables. Stir-fry for a further 5 minutes.

JAPANESE BEEF

Remember the better quality of steak used, the better the finished result will be!

Preparation time: 10 mins.　　　　*Cooking time: 15 mins.*

10-12 oz (275-350g) frying steak, rump or fillet
Salt and pepper
2 tablsp sesame seed oil
Knob fresh ginger, peeled and grated
2 tablsp soy sauce
1 tablsp clear honey
2 tablsp sherry
1 onion, peeled and chopped
8 oz (225g) fresh or frozen green beans
8 oz (225g) leeks, sliced thinly
10 oz (275g) carton beansprouts

1. Cut the meat into strips and season with salt and pepper.

2. Fry the meat quickly in the hot oil until sealed on both sides.

3. Stir in the ginger, soy sauce, honey, sherry and the vegetables.

4. Stir-fry for about 10 minutes, depending on how rare or well done you like your steak.

5. Serve with savoury rice.

COLIN'S CHICKEN STIR-FRY

Serves 4

This recipe uses half a head of Chinese leaves. Use the remainder in a salad or cook for a few minutes in boiling salted water, drain and top with a cheese sauce. Serve another night as an accompaniment to cold meat.

Preparation time: 8 mins.   *Cooking time: 10 mins*

1 tablsp sesame seed oil
1 tablsp soy sauce
½ teasp chilli powder
1 clove garlic, peeled and crushed
12 oz (350g) boneless and skinless chicken breast or
    thighs, cut into bite-size pieces
8 oz (225g) broccoli, cut into small florets 4 oz (100g)
    mushrooms, sliced
½ head Chinese leaves, sliced
1 green pepper, de-seeded and chopped
Salt and pepper

1.   Heat the oil, soy sauce and chilli powder in a wok or large frying pan.

2.   Add the garlic and chicken and stir-fry for 5 minutes.

3.   Add all the vegetables, season and stir-fry for a further 5 minutes. The vegetables should be crunchy to eat.

4.   Serve with savoury rice.

LAMB WITH GARLIC

Serves 4

Succulent pieces of lamb are cooked in their own juices with garlic, soy sauce, sherry and tooth-tender celery and cour-gettes. Serve with rice.

Preparation time: 10 mins.   *Cooking time: 20 mins.*

1 tablsp sesame seed oil
3 cloves garlic, peeled and finely chopped
1 onion, peeled and chopped
1 lb (450g) lean lamb (leg or fillet), cut into pieces
¼ teasp chilli powder
Salt and pepper
1 tablsp soy sauce
1 tablsp sherry
2 sticks celery, sliced
2 medium courgettes, cut into strips

1. Heat the oil in a wok or large frying pan, add the garlic, onion, lamb, chilli powder and seasoning and stir-fry until the meat has browned, about 5 minutes.

2. Stir in the soy sauce, sherry, celery and courgettes and cook for about 15 minutes, stirring frequently, until the meat is tender.

TURKEY AND VEGETABLE STIR-FRY   *Serves 4*

Use turkey or chicken for this quick and tasty meal. Cooked meat from a bacon joint makes a good alternative. The vegetables in this recipe are only a guide – just about any can be used. Aim for about 2 lb (900g) total weight and cook only until the vegetables are barely tender. Overcooked vegetables are just not allowed! Serve with brown rice.

Preparation time: 15 mins.   *Cooking time: 28 mins.*

4 tablsp oil
8 oz (225g) turkey OR chicken, cut in strips
1 red pepper, sliced
4 oz (100g) mushrooms, sliced
4 oz (100g) courgettes, sliced
3 spring onions, cut into pieces
3 sticks celery, sliced
8 oz (225g) broccoli, broken into small florets
8 oz (225g) carrots, cut into matchsticks
2 tablsp soy sauce

1. Heat 2 tablespoons of the oil and fry the turkey or chicken for about 8 minutes until sealed on all sides.

2. Add the remaining oil and all the prepared vegetables and fry over a medium heat for about 15 minutes, stirring frequently.

3. Add the soy sauce and continue stir-frying for a further 5 minutes.

GAMMON

Gammon makes a change and is quick and easy to cook too. Big supermarkets sell smoked tendersweet bacon chops and loin roasts, which although not cheap, are lean, full of flavour and there is no waste. The following recipes can be made using either bacon chops, loin roast (allow about 2 slices per person) or the more usual gammon steak.

BACON CHOPS WITH CREAMY MUSHROOMS
Serves 4

My son said that this was the nicest recipe in the book. A back-handed compliment perhaps seeing as his favourite foods are beefburgers and pizza! (See page 26 for serving one or two.)

Preparation time: 10 mins.   *Cooking time: 20 mins.*

4 bacon chops
1 onion, peeled and chopped
4 oz (100g) mushrooms, sliced
1 tablsp tomato purée
7 fl oz (200ml) white wine
¼ pt (150ml) double cream
Grated Parmesan cheese (optional)

1. Grill the bacon chops for about 10 minutes on each side. Transfer to a shallow ovenproof dish.

2. Meanwhile put the onion, mushrooms, tomato purée and wine in a small saucepan. Simmer until tender, about 10 minutes.

3. Boil rapidly for a further five minutes until the liquid has reduced.

4. Stir in the cream and pour the sauce over the chops.

5. If liked, sprinkle with Parmesan cheese and brown under a hot grill.

DEVILLED GAMMON

Serves 4

A variation on the perennial favourite – gammon with pine-apple. Brown sugar and mustard make the dish a little more interesting.

Preparation time: 5 mins.   *Cooking time: 20-30 mins.*

4 gammon steaks
4 teasp mustard
4 teasp soft brown sugar
8 oz (225g) can pineapple rings

1. Place the gammon on a sheet of foil in the grill pan.

2. Mix the mustard, brown sugar and a couple of table-spoons of pineapple juice together. Pour half the mixture on the gammon and grill for 10-15 minutes.

3. Turn the gammon over, pour on the remaining mixture and cook for another 10-15 minutes.

4. Top each gammon steak with a pineapple ring and trickle over the rest of the pineapple juice. Grill for a couple of minutes to heat through.

CHEESE-TOPPED GAMMON

Serves 4

Gruyère cheese imparts a more interesting flavour, but children may prefer processed cheese slices.

Preparation time: 2 mins.   *Cooking time: 30 mins.*

4 gammon steaks
8 oz (225g) can pineapple rings
Slices Gruyère or processed cheese

1. Grill the gammon for about 10-15 minutes on each side.

2. Top with a pineapple ring and cover with slices of cheese. Grill until golden and bubbly.

GAMMON INDIENNE

Serves 4

Sweet and sour with a sting!

Preparation time: 4 mins.   *Cooking time: 30 mins.*

4 gammon steaks
2 tablsp clear honey
2 tablsp orange marmalade
1 tablsp Tabasco sauce

1. Pre-heat oven to 190°C (375°F) or Gas No 5.

2. Place the gammon on foil in a shallow ovenproof dish and cook for 10 minutes.

3. Mix the honey, marmalade and Tabasco together and spoon over the gammon. Cook for a further 20 minutes.

SWEET AND SOUR BACON CHOPS

Serves 4

Baked tomatoes and buttered new potatoes make good accompaniments.

Preparation time: 4 mins.   *Cooking time: 30 mins.*

4 bacon chops or slices tendersweet loin roast
2 tablsp clear honey
1 teasp mustard
2 teasp soy sauce

1. Place the chops or loin roast on a sheet of foil in a shallow ovenproof dish.

2. Mix the honey, mustard and soy sauce together and brush half of it over the meat. Grill for 15 minutes.

3. Turn and brush on the remaining honey mixture and grill for a further 15 minutes.

GAMMON MARSALA
Serves 4

The rather sweet sherry-like liquid imparts a lovely flavour to this cream sauce.

Preparation time: 10 mins.   *Cooking time: 20-30 mins.*

4 gammon steaks
1 onion, peeled and chopped
1 clove garlic, peeled and finely chopped
4 oz (100g) mushrooms, sliced
1 tablsp cooking oil
¼ pt (150ml) Marsala
¼ pt (150ml) double cream
Salt and pepper
Chopped fresh parsley for garnish (optional)

1. Grill the gammon for about 15 minutes on each side.

2. Meanwhile, fry the onion, garlic and mushrooms in the oil until tender.

3. Add the Marsala and boil for about 5 minutes until reduced slightly. Stir in the cream and season to taste.

4. Pour the sauce over the gammon and sprinkle with chopped parsley if liked.

GAMMON WITH PLUM RELISH
Serves 4

A no-hassle tangy and fruity relish is just the thing with gammon. (See page 26 for serving one or two.)

Preparation time: 5 mins.   *Cooking time: 20 mins.*

1 onion, peeled and chopped
3 plums, halved, de-stoned and sliced
½ tablsp cooking oil

2 tablsp sultanas
2 tablsp demerara sugar
Salt and pepper
4 fl oz (100ml) red wine vinegar
4 fl oz (100ml) water
4 gammon steaks

1. Fry the onion and sliced plums gently in the oil for 5 minutes.

2. Add the sultanas, sugar, seasoning, vinegar and water.

3. Boil for about 20 minutes until the relish is thick and syrupy.

4. Meanwhile, cook the gammon steaks under a medium grill for about 8 minutes on each side.

5. Spoon over the relish and serve with new potatoes, peas and carrots.

HAM AND ASPARAGUS AU GRATIN   *Serves 4*

For economy, canned celery can be substituted for asparagus.

Preparation time: 15 mins.   *Cooking time: 20 mins.*

12 oz (340g) can asparagus spears or 1 lb 12 oz (795g)
   can celery hearts
6-8 slices cooked ham
½ pt (300ml) white sauce (see page 249) or use 1 packet
   (17g size) white sauce mix
¼ pt (150ml) asparagus or celery juice
¼ pt (150ml) milk
4 oz (100g) mature Cheddar cheese, grated
Salt and pepper

1. Pre-heat oven to 180°C (350°F) or Gas No 4.

(continued overleaf)

2. Drain the asparagus or celery, reserving the juice.

3. Divide the vegetables equally between each slice of ham and roll up. Place in a shallow ovenproof dish.

4. Make up the white sauce as per page 249 using the vegetable juice and milk, or according to manufacturer's instructions, again using juice and milk.

5. Add three quarters of the grated cheese and stir over a low heat until melted. Season to taste with salt and pepper.

6. Pour the sauce over the ham, sprinkle with the remaining cheese and bake for 20 minutes until nicely browned.

PORK, LAMB AND BEEF

PORK ROYALE   *Serves 4-6*

Everyone has their 'pet' recipe and this is mine! The dish is ideal for a dinner party if you haven't much time. The impressive result belies the time it takes to prepare and cook. The sauce can be made the night before and the cream added at the last minute. (See page 26 for serving one or two.)

Preparation time: 10 mins.   *Cooking time: 30 mins.*

1 lb-1½ lb (450g-700g) pork tenderloin
Knob butter or margarine
1 onion, peeled and chopped
6 oz (175g) mushrooms, sliced
1 tablsp cooking oil
14 oz (397g) can tomatoes, drained
2 tablsp red wine (optional)
2 beef stock cubes

¼ pt (150ml) double cream
Freshly chopped parsley for garnish (optional)

1. Pre-heat oven to 180°C (350°F) or Gas No 4.

2. Cut pork into medallions, place on a sheet of foil and dot with butter. Make a parcel with the foil and roast in oven for about 30 minutes, opening the foil for the last 5 minutes.

3. Meanwhile, fry the onion and mushrooms in the oil until tender. Drain off excess juices.

4. Add drained tomatoes (chopping them a bit in the pan), the wine (if using) and crumble in the stock cubes. Stir over a low heat until dissolved and well mixed.

5. Pour in the cream and gently shake the pan to blend with the other ingredients. Do not boil.

6. Place the pork in a shallow serving dish and pour over the sauce. Garnish with chopped parsley if liked. Serve with savoury rice or scrubbed new potatoes in their jackets, and a green vegetable.

PORK WITH CIDER SAUCE
Serves 4

For recipes of this type which are being served with a tasty sauce, you can get away with the cheaper, thinner chops. These are ideal for the busy cook because they cook more quickly.

Preparation time: 3 mins.   *Cooking time: 30 mins.*

4 thin boneless pork chops
Salt and freshly ground black pepper
1 tablsp English mustard
1-2 tablsp oil
½ pt (300ml) medium sweet cider
Chopped fresh sage for garnish (optional)

(continued overleaf)

1. Season the chops and spread a little mustard on each.

2. Fry the chops gently in the oil for about 10-15 minutes on each side. Remove to a warm serving dish.

3. Pour the cider into the pan juices and boil until reduced and thickened. Pour over the chops and garnish with chopped sage if liked.

PORK CHOPS WITH MUSTARD CREAM SAUCE
Serves 4

Chops are usually expensive so the next time you shop look for the pre-packaged ones in supermarket freezers. Admittedly they're a bit thinner than the norm, but larger and cheaper and they cook quicker too. With a little imagination you can dish up great tasting meals using cheaper chops.

Preparation time: 5 mins.   *Cooking time: 30 mins.*

4 large thin pork chops
Salt and pepper
3 tablsp cooking oil
1 clove garlic, peeled and crushed
2 teasp made English mustard OR mustard powder
¼ pt (150ml) white wine
5 fl oz (150ml) carton soured cream

1. Season the chops on both sides with salt and pepper.

2. Heat the oil in a large frying pan and add the garlic and chops.

3. Fry gently for about 15 minutes on each side until brown and well cooked. Remove the chops to a warm serving dish.

4. Drain off excess oil leaving the meat sediment in the pan.

5. Stir in the mustard and then the wine and boil for a couple of minutes.

6. Remove the pan from the heat and quickly and thoroughly stir in the soured cream. Pour the sauce over the chops.

7. Serve with green vegetables and new potatoes.

CHINESE GLAZED SPARE RIBS

Serves 4

When cooked, the ribs are crisp and the sauce thickens to form a lovely sticky glaze. Arm yourself with plenty of paper napkins and eat the ribs with your fingers.

Preparation time: 8 mins.   *Cooking time: 50 mins.*

2 lb (900g) pork spare ribs
3 tablsp cranberry sauce
2 tablsp tomato ketchup
1 tablsp soy sauce
1 tablsp Worcestershire sauce
2 tablsp clear honey
1 teasp ground ginger
1 teasp mustard
8 oz (225g) can pineapple chunks

1. Pre-heat the oven to 200°C (400°F) or Gas No 6.

2. Line a shallow ovenproof dish with foil and arrange the spare ribs on top.

3. Put all the remaining ingredients in a small pan and heat gently, stirring until smooth.

4. Pour the sauce over the ribs and cook in oven for about 50 minutes. Turn the ribs several times during cooking to make sure all parts are covered with the sauce.

PORK MANDARIN

Casseroles take rather longer to cook than other meals, because the cuts of meat are generally cheaper and therefore need longer, slower cooking. However, I like those recipes where you throw a few ingredients into a pot and it looks after itself. Use the cooking time to relax with a drink and catch up on the day's gossip with the family.

Preparation time: 10 mins.   *Cooking time: 1 hour.*

1 lb (450g) belly of pork
1 tablsp cooking oil
1 red pepper, de-seeded and sliced
14 oz (397g) can chopped tomatoes
1 cooking apple, peeled, cored and chopped
½ teasp mixed dried herbs
Salt and pepper
1 tablsp paprika pepper
11 oz (312g) can mandarin oranges, drained

1. Pre-heat oven to 170°C (325°F) or Gas No 3.

2. Trim excess fat off the pork and discard. Cut the flesh into bite-size pieces.

3. Brown the meat in the hot oil, then stir in all the other ingredients except the mandarins.

4. Bring to the boil then transfer to an ovenproof casserole and cook for about an hour until the meat is tender.

5. Stir in the drained mandarins and serve with savoury rice.

CORNED BEEF AND POTATO RISSOLES   *Serves 4*

These are a good store cupboard stand-by when children suddenly announce they want a friend to stay for tea. Adults may prefer a tangy sauce accompaniment – just heat up a can of chopped chilli tomatoes.

Preparation time: 15 mins.   *Cooking time: 10-16 mins.*

4-serving size packet instant potato
1 tablsp Worcestershire sauce
1 tablsp tomato ketchup
Salt and pepper
1 beaten egg
12 oz (340g) can corned beef, cut into small dice

1. Make up the instant potato according to manufacturer's instructions but using a little less water than stated.

2. Stir in Worcestershire sauce, ketchup and seasoning. Set aside to cool slightly.

3. Mix in the beaten egg thoroughly then gently fold in the diced corned beef.

4. Using well floured hands form the mixture into 8 patties.

5. Fry the rissoles in hot shallow oil for about 5 to 8 minutes on each side until brown.

BEAN AND CORNED BEEF HOT POT   *Serves 4*

Another favourite with children. You can either use instant mashed potato for the topping, or sliced left-over cold potato.

Preparation time: 15 mins.   *Cooking time: 20 mins.*

Packet (1½ oz/40g size) beef stew seasoning mix
½ pt (300ml) water

(continued overleaf)

1 onion, peeled and chopped
4-serving packet instant mashed potato
12 oz (340g) can corned beef, cut into cubes
16 oz (450g) can baked beans

1. Pre-heat the oven to 190°C (375°F) or Gas No 5.

2. Place beef seasoning mix, water and onion in a small saucepan. Bring to the boil, stirring all the time, until the gravy thickens. Simmer gently until the onion is tender.

3. Meanwhile, make up the instant potato according to manufacturer's instructions.

4. Stir the cubed corned beef and baked beans into the gravy, turn into an ovenproof dish and allow to cool slightly.

5. Spoon the mashed potato on top, fork up and cook in the oven for about 20 minutes until potato is nicely browned. (Brushing the potato with a little beaten egg before cooking will assist browning.) Serve with green vegetables.

LIVER WITH PEPPERCORN SAUCE   *Serves 4*

Liver is a rich form of iron although many people, including children, aren't keen. However, it is cheap and offers good value because there is no waste. Try disguising the liver with this delicious sauce!

Calf's liver is the best; tender and delicate in flavour. Lamb's liver, although a little cheaper, has a stronger flavour. Ox and pig's liver have a very pronounced flavour and are best avoided if you are trying to woo the family.

Preparation time: 5 mins.   *Cooking time: 10 mins.*

1 tablsp cooking oil
Knob butter or margarine

1 lb (450g) liver, sliced thinly
Salt and pepper
1 tablsp green peppercorns in brine, chopped
½ beef stock cube, made up with ¼ pt (150ml) water
5 fl oz (150ml) carton soured cream

1. Heat the oil with the butter or margarine in a frying pan.

2. Add the seasoned liver and chopped peppercorns and fry
    gently for about 10 minutes until the meat is cooked.
    Remove and keep warm.

3. Add the stock to the pan juices and simmer until it has
    reduced and thickened slightly.

4. Stir in the soured cream and heat to just below boiling. Pour
    over the liver and garnish with chopped parsley if liked.

GRILLED LIVER WITH CITRUS SAUCE   *Serves 4*

Liver cooks in minutes but accompanied by this delicious
tangy sauce it is designed to be savoured much longer.

Preparation time: 5 mins.   *Cooking time: 12 mins.*

1 tablsp sugar
2 tablsp wine vinegar
Juice ½ lemon
Juice 1 orange
1 stock cube made up with 8 fl oz (225ml) water
1 onion, peeled and chopped
1 lb (450g) calf's liver, thinly sliced
Wedges fresh lime for garnish (optional)
Chopped fresh sage for garnish (optional)

1. Put the sugar and vinegar in a small saucepan and cook
    over a low heat until the sugar has dissolved.

(continued overleaf)

2. Boil rapidly until mixture begins to caramelise.

3. Add lemon juice, orange juice, stock and onion and boil until the liquid has reduced by half.

4. Meanwhile grill the liver for a few minutes on each side so that the inside remains creamy in texture and pale pink in colour.

5. Arrange the liver on serving plates and pour over the fruity sauce. If liked, garnish with lime and chopped sage.

LIVER WITH MUSHROOMS
Serves 4

In this recipe liver, mushrooms and onion are cooked in mushroom soup which makes a tasty and easy sauce. Serve with noodles, rice or potatoes.

Preparation time: 5 mins.   *Cooking time: 55 mins.*

1 lb (450g) liver (any variety will do)
1 level tablsp flour
Salt and freshly ground black pepper
2 tablsp oil
1 large onion, peeled and sliced
4 oz (100g) mushrooms, sliced if large
15 oz (425g) can mushroom soup

1. Pre-heat oven to 180°C (350°F) or Gas No 4.

2. Cut the liver into pieces and coat with seasoned flour.

3. Heat the oil and brown the liver on both sides. Remove with a slotted spoon and place into an ovenproof casserole dish.

4. Fry the onion and mushrooms in the same pan for about 5 minutes, then stir in any excess flour (from coating the liver) and the soup.

5. Pour the mixture over the liver and cook for 45 minutes.

LIVER AND BACON PROVENÇAL   *Serves 4*

The traditional combination of liver and crispy bacon in a
rich tomato sauce. Serve with potatoes or boiled rice.

Preparation time: 10 mins.   *Cooking time: 1 hour*

1 lb (450g) liver (any variety will do)
2 oz (50g) flour
2 tablsp oil
8 rashers streaky bacon, each cut in 3 pieces
1 large onion, peeled and chopped
14 oz (397g) can peeled tomatoes
1 tablsp Worcestershire sauce
Salt and freshly ground black pepper
1 beef stock cube
¾ pt (425ml) water

1. Slice the liver into thick strips and coat with the flour.

2. Heat the oil and brown the liver quickly on both sides.
    Lift out with a slotted spoon and place in an ovenproof
    casserole.

3. Fry the bacon and onion in the same pan, adding more oil
    if necessary, for about 15 minutes until golden.

4. Meanwhile pre-heat oven to 180°C (350°F) or Gas No 4.

5. Stir in any excess flour (from coating the liver), toma-
    toes, Worcestershire sauce, salt, pepper, crumbled stock
    cube and water.

6. Bring to the boil and then pour the mixture over the liver.

7. Put a lid on the casserole, or cover with foil, and cook for
    45 minutes.

COLE'S KIDNEYS

Serves 4

Named after the friend who donated this tasty recipe which he often cooks for quickness after a hard day's work! Serve with rice and croûtons of fried bread.

Preparation time: 8 mins.   *Cooking time: 20 mins.*

10-12 lambs' kidneys
Knob butter or margarine
1 tablsp cooking oil
1 onion, peeled and chopped
4 oz (100g) mushrooms, sliced
1 tablsp flour
Salt and pepper
1 stock cube, made up with scant ½ pt (300ml) water
2 tablsp sherry

1. Remove skin, then slice the kidneys horizontally. Using scissors, cut out the white core and as many tubes as possible.

2. Heat the butter or margarine and the oil in a frying pan.

3. Sauté the kidneys, onion and mushrooms for about 5 minutes until the meat has browned.

4. Stir in the flour, seasoning, stock and sherry. Simmer gently for 15 minutes, stirring occasionally.

KIDNEYS À L'ORANGE

Again this recipe has a nice flavour to tempt those who turn their noses up at kidneys.

Preparation time: 15 mins.   *Cooking time: 20 mins*

8-12 lambs' kidneys, skinned, halved and cored
2 tablsp flour
Salt and pepper
½ teasp cayenne pepper
1 onion, peeled and sliced
1 tablsp cooking oil
½ beef stock cube made up with ¼ pt (150ml) water
7 oz (200g) can tomatoes
Grated rind and juice of 1 orange

1. Put the prepared kidneys, flour, salt, pepper and cayenne in a small polythene bag. Toss around to make sure the kidneys are well coated.

2. Fry the onion with the kidneys in the oil until brown on both sides.

3. Stir in any remaining flour together with the stock, tomatoes, orange rind and juice. Cover and cook gently for about 20 minutes. Serve garnished with triangles of fried bread.

SPAM FRITTERS

Serves 4

A cheap standby of years gone by. Luncheon meat or corned beef can be treated in the same way. Serve with creamed potatoes and a good mixed salad to counteract the richness.

Preparation time: 10 mins.   *Cooking time: 6 mins.*

12 oz (350g) can spam
¼ pt (150ml) fritter batter (see page 237)
Oil for deep frying

1. Cut the spam into thickish slices.

2. Make the batter as per page 237.

3. Dip the spam slices into the batter and fry in hot oil for about 6 minutes until golden brown. Drain on kitchen paper.

Tip: If using corned beef, chill the tin overnight in the fridge. The corned beef will be much easier to handle if it is hard before coating with batter.

HONEY AND MUSTARD GLAZED LAMB

Serves 4

Nothing could be easier and quicker to prepare than this honey and mustard glaze which imparts a delicious flavour to lamb. (For a single serving, use one lamb chop and a glaze made with half a teaspoon of honey and half a teaspoon of French mustard.)

Preparation time: 4 mins.   *Cooking time: 30 mins.*

4 boneless lamb chump chops
2 tablsp clear honey
2 teasp French mustard

1. Pre-heat oven to 200°C (400°F) or Gas No 6.

2. Place the chops on a sheet of foil.

3. Mix the honey and mustard together and spoon over the chops. Secure the foil in a parcel.

4. Cook for 15 minutes then open up the foil and cook for a further 15 minutes.

MEAT BALLS IN TOMATO SOUP   *Serves 4*

This quick and easy dish is a great favourite with children and is good served with noodles or rice.

Preparation time: 10 mins.   *Cooking time: 25 mins.*

12 oz (350g) minced beef
Salt and pepper
1 onion, peeled and finely chopped
1 egg, beaten
Flour
15 oz (425g) can cream of tomato soup

1. Bind the mince, seasoning, onion and egg well together, using your hand if necessary.

2. Flour your hands and form the mixture into about 14 balls. Roll each in flour.

3. Heat the soup to simmering point in a saucepan and add the meat balls. Cook gently for about 25 minutes, turning once during cooking.

CIDER BAKED SAUSAGES

Serves 4

Use good quality butcher's sausages for this recipe – nice and herby and spicy – not those mealy, tasteless supermarket jobs! Serve with scrubbed new potatoes and a watercress and orange salad.

Preparation time: 8 mins.   *Cooking time: 40 mins.*

1 lb (450g) sausages
3 sharp eating apples
1 onion, peeled and sliced
½ pt (500ml) medium sweet cider

1. Pre-heat oven to 200°C (400°F) or Gas No 6.

2. Prick the sausages and place them in an ovenproof dish.

3. Quarter, peel and core the apples and cut the flesh into slices. Put the apples and onion slices in between the sausages and pour over the cider.

4. Bake in the oven for about 40 minutes, turning the sausages, and stirring the apple and onion mixture, half-way through cooking.

N.B. Cooking time is based on thick sausages; thin ones will cook quicker. At the end, the cider and apples should have reduced to form a syrupy and fruity sauce.

ORANGE GLAZED PORK WITH VEGETABLES

Serves 4

An orange and honey marinade is brushed on the pork before cooking and also tossed through hot vegetables as a dressing. Small new potatoes or special salad potatoes, which are available at large supermarkets, are particularly good for this dish.

Preparation time: 10 mins.   *Cooking time: 20 mins.*

8 oz (225g) salad potatoes OR small new potatoes
8 oz (225g) dwarf green beans
1 lb (450g) pork tenderloin
2 tablsp cooking oil
Salt and pepper
Juice 1 orange
1 teasp clear honey
4 tomatoes, quartered

1. Cook the potatoes in boiling salted water until tender, about 20 minutes. Drain.

2. Take the bunch of dwarf beans and cut the stalks off in one go. Cook in boiling salted water until just tender, about 10 minutes.

3. Cut the pork into ½" (1cm) slices and place in a grill pan. (By lining the pan with foil first, there will be no tedious washing up!)

4. Mix the oil, seasoning, orange juice and honey together and brush the liquid liberally over the pork. Cook under a medium grill for about 8 minutes on each side, brushing frequently with the marinade.

5. Add the tomato quarters to the potatoes and beans and gently toss in the remaining marinade.

149

PORK AND APPLE PIE

Serves 4

The traditional combination of pork and apple makes a tasty pie. Serve with potatoes and vegetables in season.

Preparation time: 15 mins.   *Cooking time: 40 mins.*

1 tablsp oil
1 onion, peeled and chopped
1 lb (450g) minced pork
8 oz (225g) cooking apples, peeled, cored and sliced
1 oz (25g) flour
1 tablsp dry mustard
Salt and freshly ground black pepper
½ pt (300ml) water
8 oz (225g) short crust white or wholemeal pastry (see page 234 or use frozen, defrosted)
Milk to glaze

1. Heat the oil and fry the onion for 5 minutes.

2. Add the meat and brown quickly for a further 5 minutes.

3. Stir in the apples, flour, mustard, salt, pepper and water. Bring to the boil and then simmer for 10 minutes, stirring occasionally.

4. Pour the mixture into a pie dish and allow to cool.

5. Meanwhile, make the pastry as per page 234, unless using frozen, defrosted pastry.

6. Pre-heat oven to 190°C (375°F) or Gas No 5.

7. Roll out the pastry slightly larger than the top of the pie dish.

8. Cut off a ½" (1cm) strip from round the edge of the pastry and put this strip round the damped rim of the dish.

9. Damp the strip with water and use remaining pastry to cover the pie. Trim off excess pastry and pinch edges between thumb and forefinger.

10. Make a cross in the centre of the pie to let out steam and brush the pastry with milk.

11. Bake for about 20 minutes until the pastry has nicely browned.

POTATO AND BACON BAKE

Serves 4

An economical recipe with just a touch of indulgence!

Preparation time: 15 mins.   *Cooking time: 1 hour*

8 oz (225g) lean bacon bits, diced
Few drops oil
2 lb (900g) potatoes, peeled and sliced thinly
1 large onion, peeled and sliced thinly
Salt and freshly ground black pepper
5 fl oz (142ml) carton single cream
3 tablsp milk
2 oz (50g) mature Cheddar cheese, grated

1. Fry the bacon in the oil for 15 minutes.

2. Meanwhile, cook the potatoes and onion in boiling, salted water for 5 minutes. Drain.

3. Pre-heat oven to 180°C (350°F) or Gas No 4.

4. Layer up the potatoes and onions with the bacon in a deep ovenproof dish, sprinkling with salt and pepper in between the layers.

5. Pour on the cream and milk and top with grated cheese.

6. Bake for 45 minutes until the top is brown and crispy.

LEEK AND HAM PIE

Serves 4

Don't buy the best cans of ham for this recipe as you're only chopping it up! The ham formed from selected cuts of pork is much cheaper and just as good.

Preparation time: 20 mins.   *Cooking time: 40 mins.*

1 lb (450g) leeks, sliced
1 oz (25g) margarine
1 oz (25g) flour
3 fl oz (100ml) milk + 3 fl oz (100ml) leek water
3 oz (75g) Cheddar cheese, grated
Salt and freshly ground black pepper
7 oz (200g) can ham, diced
8 oz (225g) short crust pastry (see page 234 or
   use frozen, defrosted)

1. Cook the leeks in boiling, salted water until just tender, about 5-8 minutes. Drain but reserve the water.

2. Meanwhile, melt the margarine in a small saucepan, add the flour and cook over a low heat for 1 minute.

3. Gradually stir in the liquid (half milk and half leek water).

4. Bring to the boil, stirring all the time, and cook for a couple of minutes until the sauce has thickened.

5. Stir in the grated cheese and adjust seasoning if necessary.

6. Mix the leeks and ham into the sauce and allow to cool.

7. Pre-heat oven to 200°C (400°F) or Gas No 6.

8. Meanwhile, make the pastry as per page 234, unless using frozen, defrosted pastry.

9. Roll out half the pastry and use to line an 8" (20.5cm) shallow pie dish.

10. Spoon in the ham and leek mixture.

11. Brush the edges of the pastry with milk or water.

12. Roll out remaining pastry and cover the pie, pressing the edges together and pinching between thumb and forefinger.

13. Brush the top with milk and bake for about 30 minutes until golden brown.

PANCAKES STUFFED WITH HAM AND MUSHROOMS
Makes 8-10

Ham and mushrooms in a tasty cheese sauce is a well loved combination. Try this filling with wholemeal pancakes.

Preparation time: 10 mins.   *Cooking time: 50 mins.*

½ pt (300ml) wholemeal pancake batter (see page 236)
2 oz (50g) margarine
6 oz (175g) mushrooms, roughly chopped
1 oz (25g) flour
½ pt (300ml) milk
3 oz (75g) mature Cheddar cheese, grated
Salt and freshly ground black pepper
4 oz (100g) cooked ham, diced

1. First make the pancake batter, as per page 236.

2. Then melt the margarine in a small saucepan and gently fry the mushrooms until tender, about 10 minutes. Remove with a slotted spoon into a bowl.

3. Stir the flour into the pan juices and cook for 1 minute. Gradually add the milk and then bring to the boil, stirring until the sauce thickens.

4. Add the grated cheese and stir over a low heat until it has melted. Season to taste with salt and pepper.

5. Pre-heat oven to 180°C (350°F) or Gas No 4.

(continued overleaf)

6. Add the ham to the mushrooms and mix in a little of the cheese sauce.

7. Make and cook the pancakes as per stages 3 and 4 on page 236.

8. Divide the mixture between the pancakes, roll up and place them in a shallow ovenproof dish.

9. Pour over the remaining cheese sauce and bake for about 20 minutes until golden and bubbling.

HAM AND EGG CROQUETTES   *Makes 8*

This is a good recipe to use the last oddments of meat after boiling a bacon joint. Cooked ham could also be used. Serve with jacket potatoes and baked beans.

Preparation time: 30 mins.   *Cooking time: 5 mins.*

1½ oz (35g) margarine
1½ oz (35g) flour
¼ pt (150ml) milk
6 oz (175g) cooked ham or bacon, finely chopped
3 eggs, hard boiled and chopped
Salt and freshly ground black pepper
1 tablsp freshly chopped parsley (optional)
Beaten egg ⎫ for coating
Breadcrumbs ⎭

1. Put the margarine, flour and milk in a small saucepan and stir over a low heat until thickened.

2. Add the ham or bacon, eggs, salt, pepper and parsley if using and mix well. Allow to go cold.

3. Turn the mixture on to a floured surface, divide into 8 and roll each into a croquette shape.

4. Coat with beaten egg and then breadcrumbs.

5. Deep fry for about 5 minutes until crisp and golden brown. Drain on kitchen paper.

PARSON'S PIE   *Serves 4*

Breaking up the sausagemeat and adding tomatoes renders the filling soft and moist in texture. The pie is equally good served hot with vegetables or cold with salad.

Preparation time: 25 mins.   *Cooking time: 45 mins.*

1 large onion, peeled and chopped
1 tablsp oil
12 oz (350g) sausagemeat
14 oz (397g) can peeled tomatoes, drained
Salt and freshly ground black pepper
8 oz (225g) short crust pastry (see page 234 or use frozen, defrosted)

1. Fry the onion in the oil for about 10 minutes until lightly brown. Drain.

2. Meanwhile, put the sausagemeat into a bowl and break it up with a fork, then mix in the tomatoes, seasoning and onion.

3. Pre-heat oven to 200°C (400°F) or Gas No 6.

4. Make the pastry as per page 234, unless using frozen, defrosted.

5. Roll out half the pastry and use to line an 8" (20.5cm) shallow pie dish. Brush the edges with milk or water.

6. Spoon in the sausage mixture.

7. Roll out remaining pastry and cover the filling, pressing

(continued overleaf)

155

the edges well together. Trim off excess pastry and then pinch the edge together between thumb and fore-finger.

8. Brush the top of the pie with milk and bake for 15 minutes. Turn oven down to 180°C (350°F) or Gas No 4 and cook for a further 30 minutes.

Tip: Don't throw the tomato juice away. Use it up in soups or casseroles.

STEAK DIANE   *Serves 2*

This is rich, luxurious and expensive – but quick! If money is no object try it for a romantic dinner *à deux!*

Preparation time: 8 mins.   *Cooking time: 10-20 mins.*

2 fillet steaks (allow about 6 oz (175g) per person)
Salt
Knob butter
1 onion, peeled and chopped finely
1 tablsp black peppercorns, crushed
1 teasp Worcestershire sauce
1 tablsp lemon juice
1 tablsp brandy
4 tablsp double cream

1. Season the steak with salt. Melt the butter in a frying pan and add the onion and crushed peppercorns. Fry gently for about 5 minutes.

2. Add the steaks and fry for 5-10 minutes on each side, depending on whether they are to be rare, medium or well done.

3. Push the meat to one side and stir in the Worcestershire

sauce, lemon juice, brandy and cream. Heat gently but do not boil. Garnish with chopped fresh parsley if liked.

An equally delicious variation on the above recipe can be made by omitting the Worcestershire sauce, lemon juice and brandy and adding 3 tablespoons of Drambuie instead. Simmer the liqueur for a few minutes to reduce slightly then stir in the cream.

MEXICAN TACOS   *Serves 4*

These are very tasty, but economical because a little meat goes a long way. Serve with savoury rice and/or red kidney beans.

Preparation time: 8 mins.   *Cooking time: 20 mins.*

1 onion, peeled and chopped
1 clove garlic, peeled and finely chopped
12 oz (350g) minced beef
1 tablsp cooking oil
2 teasp Mexican chilli seasoning
10.6 oz (300g) can condensed tomato rice soup
2 tablsp water
Salt and pepper
8 taco shells
5 fl oz (150ml) carton soured cream } **for garnish**
Shredded lettuce   } **(optional)**

1. Pre-heat oven to 180°C (350°F) or Gas No 4.

2. Fry the onion, garlic and minced beef in the oil for about 10 minutes, breaking the meat up with a fork.

3. Stir in the Mexican seasoning, soup and water and simmer over a low heat for a further 10 minutes, stirring occasionally. Season to taste.

(continued overleaf)

4. Meanwhile heat the taco shells in the oven for a couple of minutes.

5. Fill the tacos with the meat mixture, top with a spoonful of soured cream and garnish with shredded lettuce.

LAMB SEVILLE   *Serves 4*

180ml bottles of tomato juice cocktail are available from most supermarkets. Use these to save time; they include Worcestershire sauce so you can omit it from the recipe. Serve with small new potatoes and salad.

Preparation time: 8 mins.   *Cooking time: 40 mins.*

4 boneless lamb chump chops or steaks
1 green pepper, de-seeded and cut into chunks
1 onion, peeled and sliced
1 heaped teasp flour
Salt and pepper
2 tablsp orange marmalade
1 teasp Worcestershire sauce
Juice 1 orange
6 fl oz (180ml) tomato juice

1. Pre-heat oven to 190°C (375°F) or Gas No 5.

2. Put chops, pepper and onion in an ovenproof dish.

3. Put the flour, seasoning and marmalade in a small bowl and gradually stir in the Worcestershire sauce, orange juice and tomato juice.

4. Pour the mixture over the chops, cover with a lid or foil and bake for about 40 minutes, until the meat is tender. (Halfway through cooking turn the chops over; and remove lid or foil for the last 10 minutes.)

PORK STROGANOFF

Serves 4

This is a delicious recipe which would do justice to a dinner party, and it won't keep you in the kitchen all night or spoil if guests are late. Serve with brown rice and lightly cooked courgettes.

Preparation time: 10 mins.   *Cooking time: 25 mins.*

1 onion, peeled and chopped
6 oz (175g) mushrooms, sliced
1 tablsp cooking oil
1 lb (450g) pork tenderloin, thinly sliced
1 tablsp flour
Salt and pepper
2 tablsp tomato purée
1 stock cube, made up with 7 fl oz (200ml) water
5 fl oz (150ml) carton soured cream
Chopped parsley for garnish (optional)

1. Fry the onion and mushrooms gently in the oil for 10 minutes.

2. Push the vegetables to the side, add the pork and cook for 5 minutes until brown on all sides.

3. Remove from heat and stir in the flour, seasoning, tomato purée and stock. Simmer gently for about 10 minutes until the meat is cooked. Stir occasionally.

4. Stir in the soured cream and serve garnished with chopped parsley if liked.

SPICY MEAT VOL-AU-VENTS   *Serves 4*

Pastry adds bulk to a meal thus making economical use of
meat. Serve these mildly spiced vol-au-vents with small new
potatoes and carrots.

Preparation time: 5 mins.   *Cooking time: 25 mins.*

4 king-size vol-au-vents
1 onion, peeled and chopped
1 small green pepper, de-seeded and diced
1 tablsp cooking oil
8 oz (225g) minced beef
1 tablsp curry paste
Packet (1½ oz/40g size) beef seasoning mix
8 fl oz (250ml) water

1. Pre-heat oven to 220°C (425°F) or Gas No 7 and cook the
    vol-au-vents for about 12 minutes until well risen and
    light brown.

2. Fry the onion and pepper in the oil for about 10 minutes.

3. Add mince, breaking it up with a fork, and brown for
    about 5 minutes.

4. Stir in the curry paste, beef seasoning mix and water.
    Simmer gently, stirring until the mixture thickens.

5. Remove the lids from the vol-au-vents and pull out and
    discard the uncooked pastry.

6. Pile the meat mixture into the vol-au-vents and pop on
    the lids.

CUMBERLAND PIE

Serves 4

This is a variation of Cottage Pie with a crunchy topping of breadcrumbs and cheese. Serve with green vegetables in season.

Preparation time: 10 mins.   *Cooking time: 30 mins.*

8 oz (225g) carrots, sliced thinly
2 tablsp oil
1 large onion, peeled and roughly chopped
1 lb (450g) minced beef
Salt and freshly ground black pepper
1 beef stock cube
14 oz (397g) can peeled tomatoes
2 lb (900g) potatoes, peeled and cut into pieces
Knob margarine or butter
Little milk
2 oz (50g) tasty Cheddar cheese, grated
2 oz (50g) fresh white breadcrumbs

1. Cook the carrots in boiling, salted water until just tender, about 8 minutes.

2. Meanwhile, heat the oil in a frying pan and sauté the onion for a few minutes until softened.

3. Add the mince, salt and pepper, roughly breaking the meat up with a fork. Cook for about 8 minutes until browned.

4. Crumble in the stock cube and add the tomatoes and drained carrots. Mix well and cook gently for a couple of minutes.

5. Turn the mixture into an ovenproof dish and allow to cool.

6. Meanwhile, cook the potatoes in boiling, salted water for about 15 minutes until tender. Drain.

7. Mash the potatoes with the margarine or butter and a little milk to a softish consistency.

(continued overleaf)

8. Pre-heat oven to 180°C (350°F) or Gas No 4.

9. Spoon the potato on to the meat mixture, flatten down with a fork, and then top with mixed grated cheese and breadcrumbs.

10. Bake for about 20 minutes until the topping is brown and crisp.

STUFFED MARROW   *Serves 4*

Marrows are really cheap in the autumn so make the most of them with this tasty stuffing.

Preparation time: 10 mins.   *Cooking time: 1 hour*

1 marrow
1 lb (450g) lean minced beef
1 onion, peeled and chopped
3 oz (75g) packet herb stuffing mix
Salt and freshly ground black pepper
1 size 3 egg, beaten
Oil for brushing

1. Peel the marrow with a sharp knife, then cut in half horizontally and scoop out the seeds.

2. Pre-heat oven to 180°C (350°F) or Gas No 4.

3. Mix the meat, onion, stuffing mix, salt, pepper and beaten egg together and press the mixture into the hollows in the two marrow halves.

4. Brush the marrow with oil, wrap in foil and bake for 1 hour.

CORNED BEEF HASH

It's hard to believe that ready-prepared versions of this basic meal are on the market, neatly surrounded by a glossy photograph! This tasty combination of corned beef, tomatoes and onion is topped with fluffy potato, and a family size serving costs a few pence more than one meagre convenience portion! It's quick to do too. Serve with vegetables or salad.

Preparation time: 15 mins.   *Cooking time: 35 mins.*

2 lb (900g) potatoes, peeled and cut into pieces
½ tablsp oil
1 large onion, peeled and chopped
12 oz (350g) can corned beef
14 oz (397g) can peeled tomatoes
Salt and freshly ground black pepper
4 tablsp milk
1 size 3 egg, beaten

1. Cook the potatoes in boiling, salted water for about 10 minutes until tender. Drain.

2. Heat the oil and sauté the onion for a few minutes until transparent. Lift out with a slotted spoon and put in a bowl.

3. Add the corned beef, tomatoes (with their juice), salt and pepper to the onion and mix well. Turn the mixture into an ovenproof dish.

4. Pre-heat oven to 200°C (400°F) or Gas No 6.

5. Mash the potatoes, then beat in the milk and beaten egg to make a soft fluffy consistency.

6. Spoon the potato on top of the corned beef mixture and level off with a fork.

7. Cook for about 25 minutes until the potato is brown and crispy.

CORNISH PASTIES

A tasty mixture of meat, potatoes and onion, these pasties are good served hot or cold with vegetables or salad.

Preparation time: 30 mins.   *Cooking time: 1 hour*

8 oz (225g) short crust pastry (see page 234 or use frozen, defrosted)
8 oz (225g) potatoes, diced
1 onion, peeled and chopped
8 oz (225g) chuck or braising steak, cut into small pieces
1 beef stock cube
Salt and freshly ground black pepper
1 tablsp water
Milk to glaze pastry

1. Pre-heat oven to 200°C (400°F) or Gas No 6.

2. Make the pastry as per page 234, unless using frozen, defrosted.

3. Mix the potatoes, onion, meat, crumbled stock cube, salt, pepper and water together.

4. Roll out the pastry and then, using a saucer or plate about 6" (15cm) in diameter, cut out 4 rounds. (You will probably have to roll out the scraps to get the fourth round.)

5. Divide the meat mixture between the pastry rounds, brush the edges with milk and then fold over, crimping the edges firmly between thumb and forefinger.

6. Place the pasties on a greased baking tray and brush the tops with milk.

7. Bake for 12 minutes then turn the oven down to 170°C (325°F) or Gas No 3 and cook for a further 45-50 minutes.

RISSOLES

Serves 4

Any cold cooked meat can be used to make rissoles.

Preparation time: 20 mins.   *Cooking time: 30 mins.*

1 lb (450g) potatoes, peeled and cut into pieces
8 oz (225g) cold cooked beef
1 onion, peeled and grated
1 tablsp Worcestershire sauce
Salt and freshly ground black pepper
1 size 2 egg, beaten

1. Cook the potatoes in boiling, salted water until tender, about 12-15 minutes. Drain and then mash.

2. Meanwhile, mince or finely chop the meat.

3. Mix the mashed potato, meat, onion, Worcestershire sauce, salt, pepper and egg and bind well.

4. Divide mixture into 4, roll each in flour and press into patties about ½" (1cm) thick.

5. Shallow fry for 10-15 minutes on each side.

165

11   POULTRY

Chicken and turkey are good sources of protein, contain little fat and offer good value for money. It is essential that poultry is cooked thoroughly; test by piercing with a skewer – the juices that run out should be clear. Larger chicken joints which contain a bone don't shallow fry very well because of their uneven thickness and non-uniform shape. Such joints are better cooked in a medium oven for about 45 minutes. Thin turkey escallops are also well worth buying.

Cuts containing a bone are cheaper, and although you can use them in the following recipes, cooking times will need to be extended. Chicken can be combined with an infinite variety of ingredients to make interesting meals and offers endless possibilities for experimenting with different flavours.

CHICKEN À L'ORANGE

Serves 4

Garlicky orange butter renders the chicken moist and flavourful. Serve with wild rice and mixed salad. Depending on appetite, allow 2-3 chicken thighs per person.

Preparation time: 8 mins.   *Cooking time: 25 mins.*

8-12 boneless and skinless chicken thighs
1 tablsp butter or margarine
2 cloves garlic, peeled and finely chopped
1 tablsp flour
1 teasp soft brown sugar
Salt and pepper
Grated rind and juice of 1 orange

1. Pre-heat oven to 200°C (400°F) or Gas No 6.

2. Using a sharp knife, score each chicken piece with three deep cuts.

3. In a small bowl combine the butter or margarine, garlic, flour, sugar, seasoning, orange rind and one tablespoon of juice.

4. Using a round-bladed knife fill the cuts in the chicken with the butter mixture.

5. Place the chicken close together in a shallow ovenproof dish and pour over the remaining orange juice. Cook for about 25 minutes.

MEXICAN HONEYED CHICKEN *Serves 4*

When cooked, the honey crisps to a sticky glaze, its sweetness offset by the chilli powder. (For a single serving, use two or three chicken thighs and make the glaze with 1 tablespoon of honey and half a teaspoon of chilli powder.)

Preparation time: 5 mins.   *Cooking time: 25 mins.*

8-12 boneless and skinless chicken thighs
4 tablsp clear honey
2 teasp chilli powder
Salt and pepper

1. Pre-heat oven to 200°C (400°F) or Gas No 6.

2. Using a sharp knife, score each chicken piece with three deep cuts.

3. In a small bowl blend the honey, chilli powder, salt and pepper.

4. Place the chicken close together in a shallow ovenproof dish. Spoon the honey mixture into the cuts.

5. Bake in the oven for about 25 minutes.

TURKEY CAPPARIS

Serves 4

Named after the caper, a bramble-like Mediterranean shrub, whose flower buds are pickled for culinary use. You could use green peppercorns in brine instead of capers – either one imparts a sharp bite to the bland creamy sauce. (See page 26 for serving one or two.)

Preparation time: 5 mins. *Cooking time: 20 mins.*

Knob butter or margarine
1 tablsp cooking oil
2 tablsp capers or green peppercorns in brine
Salt and pepper
4 turkey escallops
1 teasp flour
¼ pt (150ml) white grape juice
2 tablsp double cream

1. Heat the butter or margarine with the oil in a large frying pan and toss in the capers or peppercorns.

2. Season the turkey and brown quickly on both sides.

3. Stir in the flour to the pan juices and pour in the grape juice.

4. Simmer gently until the turkey is cooked, about 8 minutes each side. The liquid should have thickened; if it hasn't, continue cooking for a further few minutes.

5. Stir in the cream and adjust seasoning if necessary.

CHICKEN TERYAKI *Serves 4*

The sauce cooks to a syrupy glaze which nicely complements
the delicate flavour of chicken.

Preparation time: 5 mins.   *Cooking time: 20 mins.*

Knob butter or margarine
1 tablsp cooking oil
2 teasp sesame seeds
3-4 boneless and skinless chicken breasts
1 teasp soft brown sugar
1 tablsp clear honey
2 tablsp soy sauce
Juice 1 lemon
Knob fresh ginger, peeled and coarsely grated

1. Heat the butter or margarine with the oil in a large frying
   pan, add the sesame seeds and fry for a few seconds until
   brown.

2. Cut the chicken into diagonal slices. Add to the pan and
   brown quickly on both sides.

3. Stir in the sugar, honey, soy sauce, lemon juice and
   ginger.

4. Simmer for about 15-20 minutes, turning the chicken
   occasionally. The liquid should by syrupy. Serve with
   pilau rice and a watercress and orange salad.

TANDOORI CHICKEN

Serves 4

This mildly spiced dish is a perennial favourite. The chicken should be brown and crusty on the outside and moist inside. Naan bread and a mixed salad make ideal accompaniments. (See page 26 for serving one or two.)

Preparation time: 5 mins.   *Cooking time: 30 mins.*

8-12 boneless and skinless chicken thighs
5 fl oz (150ml) Greek yoghurt
Juice 1 lemon
2 cloves garlic, peeled and very finely chopped
1 teasp garam masala
1 teasp paprika
1 teasp turmeric
2 teasp ground coriander
Salt and pepper
Chopped fresh coriander for garnish (optional)

1. Pre-heat oven to 200°C (400°F) or Gas No 6.

2. Make several deep cuts in the chicken pieces.

3. Combine all the remaining ingredients except the fresh coriander.

4. Put the chicken in a shallow ovenproof dish and spoon over the marinade, rubbing it well into the cuts.

5. Bake for 30 minutes until the chicken is tender and garnish with chopped coriander if liked.

LEMON FRIED CHICKEN

Serves 4

Slivers of chicken are deep fried in a lemon crumb coating. Serve with a mayonnaise-based dip.

Preparation time: 15 mins. *Cooking time: 8 mins.*

8 boneless and skinless chicken thighs
1 egg, beaten
1 tablsp self-raising flour
5 tablsp breadcrumbs
1 teasp turmeric
2 teasp ground coriander
Salt and pepper
Finely grated rind 1 lemon

1. Cut the chicken into thin strips.

2. Toss the chicken in the beaten egg.

3. Put the flour, breadcrumbs, turmeric, coriander, seasoning and lemon rind in a small polythene bag. Add the chicken in two or three batches and shake the bag until the chicken is well coated with the mix.

4. Fry in deep hot oil for about 8 minutes until golden brown and cooked through. Drain on kitchen paper.

5. Serve squeezed with lemon juice, using the lemon from which the rind was grated.

CURRIED HAWAIIAN TURKEY

Serves 4

This is a simple no-hassle dish to prepare. The combination of curry powder and pineapple complements turkey or chicken particularly well. It is not at all hot and spicy and I find the flavour appeals to children.

Preparation time: 6 mins.   *Cooking time: 25 mins.*

2 tablsp cooking oil
1 onion, peeled and chopped
Salt and pepper
4 turkey escallops
1 tablsp flour
2 tablsp mild curry powder
1 stock cube, made up with 7 fl oz (200ml) water
15 oz (400g) can crushed pineapple

1. Heat the oil in a large frying pan and add the onion.

2. Season the turkey escallops and place them on top of the onion. Fry gently for five minutes on each side.

3. Mix the flour and curry powder together, sprinkle over the escallops and turn them over.

4. Add stock and crushed pineapple with juice.

5. Simmer for about 15 minutes, turning the escallops over once. If the sauce becomes too thick during cooking, add a dash of water.

DEVILLED CHICKEN DRUMSTICKS   *Serves 4*

This tasty oily marinade is ideal for using on meat which is to be barbequed. Serve the drumsticks with salad and garlic bread. (For a single serving use about two drumsticks and make up the marinade with 1 tablespoon of oil, a shake of paprika and ginger and half a teaspoon of mustard powder. If, when you come to make the dish again, a more distinctive flavour is preferred, simply add more of the spices.)

Preparation time: 5 mins.   *Cooking time: 40 mins.*

8 chicken drumsticks
4 fl oz (100ml) cooking oil
Salt and pepper
1 teasp paprika
1 teasp powdered ginger
2 teasp mustard powder

1. Pre-heat oven to 200°C (400°F) or Gas No 6.

2. Using a sharp knife make three or four slashes in each drumstick and place them close together in a shallow ovenproof dish.

3. Combine the remaining ingredients in a small screw top jar and shake until well mixed.

4. Pour the liquid over the chicken and cook for about 40 minutes, basting frequently.

CHICKEN AND HAM VOL-AU-VENTS   *Serves 4*

Condensed soups make instant sauces and can be combined with left-over meat and vegetables for tasty pastry fillings.

Preparation time: 8 mins.   *Cooking time: 17 mins.*

4 king-size vol-au-vents
Handful of frozen peas
4 oz (100g) cooked chicken, diced
4 oz (100g) cooked ham, diced
Freshly ground black pepper
10.4 oz (295g) can condensed chicken soup

1. Pre-heat oven to 220°C (425°F) or Gas No 7 and cook the vol-au-vents for about 12 minutes until well risen and light brown.

2. Meanwhile, put the peas in a bowl, pour on boiling water and leave until the vol-au-vents are cooked, then drain.

3. Mix the chicken, ham, black pepper, soup and drained peas together.

4. Remove the lids from the vol-au-vents and pull out uncooked pastry and discard.

5. Fill the vol-au-vents with the chicken mixture, pop on the pastry lids and heat in the oven for about 5 minutes.

CHICKEN CURRY

Serves 4

Serve with white or brown rice.

Preparation time: 15 mins.   *Cooking time: 1 hour*

2 tablsp oil
4 chicken pieces
1 onion, peeled and chopped
1 green pepper, cut into chunks
1 red pepper, cut into chunks
2 medium sized potatoes, peeled and cut into chunks
1 level tablsp curry powder or more to taste
1 stock cube
14 oz (397g) can peeled tomatoes
½ pt (300ml) water

1. Heat the oil and brown the chicken on all sides. Remove to a lidded ovenproof casserole dish.

2. Fry the onion, peppers and potatoes for about 10 minutes, adding more oil if necessary. Lift out with a slotted spoon and add to the casserole.

3. Pre-heat oven to 180°C (350°F) or Gas No 4.

4. Stir the curry powder and crumbled stock cube into the pan juices, then add the tomatoes and water.

5. Bring to the boil and then pour into the casserole dish.

6. Cook for about 1 hour until the chicken is tender.

See also: Colin's Chicken Stir-Fry, page 126
         Turkey and Vegetable Stir-Fry, page 128.

12   SOUPS

Home-made soups have enjoyed something of a renaissance in recent years – and rightly so! They are cheap and easy to prepare; wholesome and filling to eat. This chapter includes hearty varieties which are designed to be meals in themselves.

One of the nicest accompaniments is fresh crusty bread and butter, but there are others which add bulk and flavour. These include small dumplings, croûtons, crispy bacon, cheese, pearl barley, rice and pasta (such as noodles and macaroni).

Dumplings: See page 232.

Croûtons: Cut slices of bread (stale is ideal) into small cubes and either shallow fry in a little oil and melted margarine or deep fry in a chip pan until golden brown. Drain on kitchen paper.

Bacon: Grill bacon rashers until crisp, then crumble roughly and sprinkle over the soup.

Cheese: Grated Parmesan, Cheddar or other similar hard cheese can be sprinkled on top of the soup, particularly vegetable varieties.

Pearl Barley: Add about 2 oz (50g) to the soup at the beginning of cooking. It goes well with vegetable broths.

Rice: Left-over cooked rice can be added to the soup a couple of minutes before the end of cooking. Alternatively, add uncooked rice to the soup, allowing 15 minutes' cooking time. Tomato soup and rice is a good combination.

Noodles: Cook in the soup for about 10 minutes. Noodles are especially good with chicken, or any of the thinner soups.

Macaroni: Again, good with any thin vegetable soup such as minestrone. Use the thin macaroni and allow about 15 minutes' cooking time.

STOCK

Soup can be made with water and ready-made stock cubes but the most flavour and nourishment is gained from using home-made stock (see page 251).

FRENCH ONION SOUP   *Serves 4*

Traditionally Gruyère cheese is used in this recipe but Cheddar is cheaper and gives good results.

Preparation time: 5 mins.   *Cooking time: 40 mins.*

2 oz (50g) margarine
1½ lb (700g) onions, peeled and sliced
1 level tablsp flour
1½ pts (850ml) meat or vegetable stock
4 slices French bread
2 oz (50g) mature Cheddar cheese, grated

1. Heat the margarine in a saucepan until it is foaming and then fry the onion for about 15-20 minutes until light brown.

2. Stir in the flour and cook for a couple of minutes.

3. Gradually add the stock, stirring all the time, bring to the

178

boil and then simmer for 20 minutes. Adjust seasoning if necessary.

4. Divide the soup between 4 bowls, put a slice of French bread on each and top with the grated cheese.

5. Pop under a hot grill for a couple of minutes until the cheese is bubbling.

LEEK AND POTATO SOUP

Serves 4

As with many thick cream-style soups, the mixture should be puréed to give professional results. The use of an electric blender or food processor is therefore a distinct advantage. Failing these, rub the finished soup through a sieve.

Preparation time: 10 mins.   *Cooking time: 35 mins.*

1 oz (25g) margarine
1 lb (450g) leeks, sliced
2 medium sized potatoes, peeled and diced
2 pts (1.1 litres) vegetable or chicken stock
Salt and freshly ground black pepper

1. Melt the margarine in a large saucepan and gently fry the leeks and potatoes for 5 minutes.

2. Add the stock, bring to the boil and simmer for about 30 minutes until the potatoes are tender.

3. Purée the soup in a blender or rub through a sieve.

4. Re-heat the soup and add salt and pepper if necessary.

179

CREAM OF CELERY SOUP

Serves 4

For best results use the celery heart only. The outer stalks can be added to casseroles or used to make stock.

Preparation time: 10 mins.   *Cooking time: 40 mins.*

2 oz (50g) margarine
1 celery heart, chopped
2 oz (50g) flour
1½ pts (850ml) vegetable or chicken stock
½ pt (300ml) milk
Salt and freshly ground black pepper

1. Melt the margarine and gently fry the chopped celery for 8 minutes.

2. Stir in the flour and cook for a further minute.

3. Gradually stir in the stock and milk and then bring to the boil, stirring all the time.

4. Simmer for 30 minutes, stirring occasionally. Add salt and pepper to taste if necessary.

CREAM OF MUSHROOM SOUP

Serves 4

Anyone who is new to soup-making could do no better than to start with a cream-style soup. This recipe is easy and delicious.

Preparation time: 10 mins.   *Cooking time: 40 mins.*

3 oz (75g) margarine
6 oz (175g) mushrooms, thinly sliced
1 small onion, peeled and finely chopped
2 oz (50g) flour
1½ pts (850ml) vegetable or chicken stock

½ pt (300ml) milk
Salt and freshly ground black pepper

1. Melt the margarine and gently fry the mushrooms and onion for 8 minutes.

2. Stir in the flour and cook for a further minute.

3. Gradually stir in the stock and milk, bring to the boil stirring all the time, and then simmer for 30 minutes.

4. Season to taste with salt and pepper.

LENTIL SOUP WITH CRISPY BACON   *Serves 4-6*

To make a really hearty meal, cook small dumplings in the soup after it has been puréed (see page 232). Then top with the crispy bacon just before serving.

Preparation time: 10 mins.   *Cooking time: 40 mins.*

6 oz (175g) split red lentils, washed
8 oz (225g) potatoes, peeled and diced
2 pts (1.1 litres) meat, chicken or vegetable stock
Salt and freshly ground black pepper
4-6 rashers streaky bacon

1. Put the lentils, potatoes, stock and a little salt and pepper in a large saucepan. Bring to the boil and simmer for 40 minutes.

2. Meanwhile, grill the bacon until really crispy and leave to cool.

3. Purée the soup in a blender or rub through a sieve.

4. Return the soup to the saucepan to re-heat, pour into individual bowls and then crumble the bacon on top.

181

13 TELEVISION SUPPERS, SNACKS AND SALADS

This chapter aims for the bistro or wine-bar style snack, ideal for days when you don't feel like a hearty meal.

For instance there are times when all families like to huddle round the fire, watching a favourite television programme, with a fork in one hand and something tasty to eat in the other.

In summer something light and cool is welcome, an all-in-one-salad perhaps, which can be served with chunks of fresh bread and butter and enjoyed in the garden.

STUFFED PÂTÉ MUSHROOMS   *Serves 4*

These are rich and delicious; hot garlic bread and a salad of
shredded lettuce, watercress, cucumber and tomato make
good accompaniments. A vegetarian stuffing could be made
by using mushroom pâté.

Preparation time: 15 mins.   *Cooking time: 10 mins.*

8 large flat mushrooms
Cooking oil
6 oz (175g) good quality smooth pâté
2 tablsp medium sherry
Juice 1 lemon
4 tablsp herb and garlic stuffing mix
1 teasp chopped fresh rosemary (optional)

1. Pre-heat oven to 200°C (400°F) or Gas No 6.

2. Remove mushroom stalks and reserve. Put the caps in a
    roasting tin and pour in enough oil to cover the base.
    Brush mushrooms liberally with the oil.

3. Mix pâté, sherry, lemon juice, stuffing mix and rosemary
    well together. Spoon the mixture on to the mushrooms
    and replace the stalks.

4. Brush again with oil, bake in the oven for 10 minutes and
    serve immediately.

HOT CREAM CHEESE WITH PRAWNS   *Serves 4*

This recipe was cadged from my local wine bar! You can eat
it like pâté on melba toast, crackers or chunks of fresh bread.
Serve with a salad garnish of celery and carrot sticks.

Preparation time: 5 mins.   *Cooking time: 3 mins.*

14 oz (400g) cream cheese
1 tablsp French mustard

(continued overleaf)

2 spring onions, chopped
4 oz (100g) peeled prawns
Grated Parmesan cheese

1. Pre-heat oven to 220°C (425°F) or Gas No 7.

2. Mix the cream cheese, mustard, spring onions and prawns well together and press into 4 individual oven-proof dishes, sprinkle liberally with grated Parmesan and pop in the oven for a few minutes.

SUMMER BEEF SALAD   *Serves 4*

This is a good way of using up cold beef from a roast joint. Alternatively you can buy cold sliced beef from a delicatessen or supermarket. The parsley is an essential ingredient to the flavour so use it if you can. Serve with fresh crusty bread.

Preparation time: 15 mins.   *Cooking time: None.*

12 oz (350g) cold roast beef
1 eating apple, peeled, cored and diced
½ cucumber, peeled and diced
2 celery sticks, sliced
1 bunch parsley, chopped
2 tablsp olive oil
Juice 1 lemon
1 tablsp soy sauce

1. Cut the beef into strips and mix with the apple, cucumber, celery and parsley.

2. Mix the oil, lemon juice and soy sauce together. (A screwtop jar is ideal for making liquid dressings as all the ingredients can be shaken well together.)

3. Fold the dressing through the beef mixture and turn into a serving dish.

POTTED SHRIMPS

These make a tasty light snack or a quick starter for a dinner party. Serve with thin slices of toast. Allow 30 minutes chilling time before eating.

Preparation time: 3 mins.   *Cooking time: 5 mins.*

7 oz (200g) can shrimps, drained
3 oz (75g) butter
1 teasp paprika
Dash cayenne (optional)
Freshly ground black pepper
Wedges of lemon and salad greens for garnish

1. Heat the shrimps and butter together in a small saucepan for a few minutes.

2. Stir in the paprika, cayenne (if using) and black pepper and cook gently for a couple of minutes.

3. Press the mixture into 4 individual pots and chill for about 30 minutes until solidified.

4. Turn out on to small plates and garnish with wedges of lemon and salad greens.

AVOCADO WITH SPICY TUNA
Serves 4

The piquant tuna mixture goes really well with the bland flavour of avocados. Serve with garlic bread and green salad.

Preparation time: 15 mins.   *Cooking time: None.*

7 oz (200g) can tuna fish, drained
3 tablsp mayonnaise
3 teasp Worcestershire sauce
2 teasp tomato purée

(continued overleaf)

Juice ½ lemon
1 small onion, peeled and finely chopped
Salt and black pepper
4 avocado pears

1. Roughly flake the tuna into a bowl and add all the ingredients except the pears.

2. Halve and peel the avocados and discard the stones. Slice pears so that the halves fan out on the plate. Pile the tuna mixture in the centre and sprinkle with a little cayenne pepper if liked. Garnish with shredded lettuce.

AVOCADO AND BACON SALAD   *Serves 4*

Another tasty avocado salad. Use a dressing of your choice – mild curry, thousand island, blue cheese or herb and garlic are all good. Alternatively, soured cream and chopped chives go well with bacon.

Preparation time: 10 mins.   *Cooking time: 15 mins.*

12 oz (350g) smoked streaky bacon, diced
4 avocados
Mixed salad
4 generous tablsp mayonnaise-based dressing

1. Fry the diced bacon until crisp, about 15 minutes.

2. Meanwhile, halve, peel and de-stone the avocados. Avocado flesh discolours when exposed to the air. If you are preparing this dish more than about 40 minutes before eating, it is advisable to brush lemon juice on the cut edges.

3. Arrange a salad on 4 individual plates and place the avocados on top, cut side down.

4. Spoon the dressing over the avocados and top with crispy bacon.

PRAWN AND SWEETCORN TOAST TOPPER

Serves 4

For a 'hot' version add a good shake of cayenne pepper to the mixture. Serve with thin slices of toast and a salad garnish.

Preparation time: 10 mins.   *Cooking time: 15 mins.*

2 eggs, hardboiled
7 fl oz (200ml) white sauce (see page 249 or use 1 packet
  (17g size) white sauce mix)
4 oz (100g) peeled prawns
7 oz (200g) can sweetcorn, drained
4 oz (100g) mature Cheddar cheese, grated

1. While the eggs are boiling make up the white sauce as per page 249 but only use 7 fl oz (200ml) milk – other quantities as per recipe. (If using white sauce mix, make up as per manufacturer's instructions but only use 7 fl oz (200ml) milk.)

2. Stir in the prawns, sweetcorn and three quarters of the cheese.

3. Peel and chop the eggs and stir into the sauce. Spoon the mixture into 4 heatproof dishes, top with remaining cheese and brown under a hot grill for about 5 minutes.

Grilled or fried sandwiches make tasty quick snacks which satisfy the heartiest appetite. Sliced bread, pittas, halved rolls or split French sticks are suitable for a variety of fillings or toppings. I'm sure you can create your own combinations but here are a few ideas to start you off. Snacks like these are good during the school holidays – older children could even make their own.

CROQUE MONSIEUR

Serves 4

Just about any cheese is suitable, from processed cheese slices to Mozzarella. I particularly like the latter because it goes deliciously gooey and stringy when cooked.

Preparation time: 10 mins.   *Cooking time: 8 mins.*

Butter or margarine
8 slices medium sliced bread
4 slices cooked ham
Slices of cheese – Cheddar, Gruyère or Mozzarella

1. Butter each slice of bread on one side only.

2. With the butter side out, sandwich together in pairs with a slice of ham and some cheese.

3. Grill gently for about 4 minutes on each side until the cheese has melted and the bread is golden brown.

EGG AND BACON TOASTIES

Serves 4

Preparation time: 10 mins.   *Cooking time: 15 mins.*

6 rashers smoked streaky bacon, diced
3 eggs
2 tablsp mayonnaise
Salt and pepper
4-6 slices buttered toast
Slices of tomato (optional)

1. Grill or fry the diced bacon until crisp.

2. Hardboil the eggs then peel and chop.

3. Mix the bacon, eggs, mayonnaise and seasoning together and spread on buttered toast.

4. Top with slices of tomato, if liked, and pop under a hot grill for a minute to brown. Cut into triangles.

CHEESE AND PINEAPPLE TOASTIES   *Serves 4*

Preparation time: 10 mins.   *Cooking time: 5 mins.*

4 slices cooked ham, diced
4 oz (100g) mature Cheddar cheese, grated
2 tablsp canned crushed pineapple
4-6 slices buttered toast

> Mix the ham, cheese and pineapple together. Spread the mixture on buttered toast and pop under a medium grill until golden and bubbly.

SAVOURY PITTAS   *Serves 4*

Pitta bread makes a good base for all types of tasty toppings. Use left-overs or bits and pieces from the store cupboard and top with slices of cheese.

Preparation time: 10 mins.   *Cooking time: 5 mins.*

Handful of dried sliced mushrooms
4 individual pittas
2 sun-dried tomatoes OR ½-1 tablsp tomato purée
8 slices salami
Slices Mozzarella cheese

1. Put the mushrooms in a cup and pour on boiling water. Leave for 10 minutes.

2. Smear the pitta bread with sun-dried tomatoes or tomato purée.

3. Top with salami, the drained mushrooms and cheese.

4. Pop under a medium grill for about 5 minutes until the cheese is gooey.

TOASTED CHEESE AND TUNA ROLLS   *Serves 4*

Preparation time: 10 mins.   *Cooking time: 5 mins.*

4 baps
7 oz (200g) can tuna fish, drained
7 oz (200g) can sweetcorn, drained
3 tablsp mayonnaise
2 oz (50g) mature Cheddar cheese, grated

1.   Split the baps in half.

2.   Mix the tuna, corn, mayonnaise and cheese together. Pile
     the mixture on the rolls and grill for about 5 minutes.

BAKED BRIE WITH APPLES AND ALMONDS
Serves 4

A new angle on plain old cheese and biscuits. This is another
wine-bar recipe and is lovely served with buttered crackers or
chunks of wholemeal bread.

Preparation time: 5 mins.   *Cooking time: 4 mins.*

4 pieces fresh Brie
2 tablsp flaked almonds
2 sharp eating apples, quartered, cored and sliced

1.   Pre-heat oven to 220°C (425°F) or Gas No 7.

2.   Put the pieces of Brie on four individual ovenproof plates
     and sprinkle some nuts over each.

3.   Pop into the oven for about 4 minutes until the cheese has
     slightly melted and the nuts browned.

4.   Arrange the sliced apples down on one side of the cheese
     and the crackers or bread on the other.

ITALIAN SALAD

For a more substantial meal, add a few rolled up anchovies and some sliced salami. Serve with one of the more unusual varieties of lettuce like Lollo Rosso, Quattro Stagioni or Radicchio (a red leafed Italian chicory). All are usually available from larger supermarkets. Hot garlic bread is also a delicious accompaniment.

Preparation time: 15 mins.   *Cooking time: None.*

1 lb (450g) beefsteak tomatoes
4 oz (100g) Mozzarella cheese
1 small onion
7 oz (200g) can sweet red peppers, drained
Few black olives, stoned
2 teasp chopped fresh basil OR 1 teasp dried
4 tablsp olive oil
Juice 1 lemon
1 tablsp white wine vinegar
Pinch sugar
Salt and pepper

1. Slice the tomatoes and cheese and arrange in a shallow dish.

2. Peel and cut the onion into wafer thin slices.

3. Cut the peppers into strips.

4. Arrange the onion, peppers and olives on top of the cheese and tomatoes.

5. Put the basil, oil, lemon juice, vinegar, sugar and seasoning into a screw-top jar and shake well until thick. Pour the dressing over the salad.

WALDORF SALAD WITH PEACHES   *Serves 4*

This is a variation on a classic salad using fresh peaches as well as apples. Served on its own it makes an ideal light summer supper, but for a more substantial meal accompany with fresh bread and a selection of cheese.

Preparation time: 20 mins.   *Cooking time: 5 mins.*

8 oz (225g) dwarf green beans
1 red eating apple
1 green eating apple
2 fresh peaches
1 stick celery
2 oz (50g) walnut pieces
5 oz (150g) carton natural yoghurt
2 tablsp mayonnaise
Juice 1 orange

1. Cook the beans in boiling salted water for about 5 minutes, until just tender. Drain.

2. Quarter the apples, remove cores and slice the flesh into a bowl.

3. Halve the peaches, remove stones and slice the flesh into the bowl.

4. Thinly slice the celery and add to the bowl together with the walnuts and drained beans.

5. Combine the yoghurt, mayonnaise and orange juice and fold through the fruit and vegetable mixture.

PRAWN COCKTAIL VOL-AU-VENTS   *Serves 4*

These make a tasty quick summer supper. Serve with mixed salad and some sliced chicory tossed in vinaigrette dressing.

Preparation time: 8 mins.   *Cooking time: 12 mins.*

4 king-size frozen vol-au-vents
8 oz (225g) peeled prawns
2 tablsp tomato purée or ketchup
4 tablsp mayonnaise
Ground black pepper
Shredded lettuce
Lemon wedges for garnish (optional)

1. Pre-heat oven to 200°C (425°F) or Gas No 7. Cook the vol-au-vents for about 12 minutes until well risen and lightly brown. Allow to cool slightly.

2. Meanwhile mix the prawns, tomato purée or ketchup, mayonnaise and black pepper together.

3. Remove the lids from the vol-au-vents and pull out uncooked pastry and discard.

4. Half fill the vol-au-vents with shredded lettuce then fill with the prawn mixture and pop back the pastry lids. Garnish with lemon wedges if liked.

HOT PITTA POCKETS

If you slit open pitta bread it forms a natural pocket which can be stuffed with a variety of tasty fillings. No doubt you will devise your own combinations but here are two delicious recipes to give you an idea. Quantities given are enough for 6-8 mini, or 4-6 large pittas, depending on how much filling you want to put in. The stuffed pittas are wrapped in foil and

(continued overleaf)

cooked in a hot oven for a few minutes. Serve with a selection of raw vegetables – carrot and celery sticks, chunks of tomato and cucumber and chicory leaves are all ideal.

MEXICAN PITTAS   *Serves 4*

Preparation time: 8 mins.   *Cooking time: 7 mins.*

Pitta bread
8 oz (225g) sliced salami
15 oz (425g) can red kidney beans, drained
6 tablsp garlic mayonnaise
Few drops Tabasco sauce (optional)

1. Pre-heat oven to 200°C (400°F) or Gas No 6.

2. Split the pitta bread to form a pocket and line with slices of salami.

3. Mix the beans, mayonnaise and Tabasco sauce together and spoon into the pitta bread.

4. Wrap each individually in foil and bake for about 7 minutes.

CREAM CHEESE AND BACON PITTAS   *Serves 4*

Preparation time: 8 mins.   *Cooking time: 17 mins.*

6 oz (175g) smoked streaky bacon
8 oz (225g) cream cheese
1 tomato, chopped
Freshly ground black pepper
Few chopped chives (optional)
Pitta bread

1. Pre-heat the oven to 200°C (400°F) or Gas No 6.

2. Grill the bacon until crisp, about 10 minutes, then roughly chop it.

3. Mix the bacon, cream cheese, tomato, pepper and chives together.

4. Split the pitta bread to form a pocket and stuff with the cheese mixture.

5. Wrap each individually in foil and bake for about 7 minutes.

SAVOURY CHOUX BUNS   *Makes 4*

Contrary to popular belief, choux pastry is quick and easy and makes a useful base for savoury and sweet dishes. (See also chapter on Desserts.) Choux buns are airy in texture, just the thing for a luxury filling of cream cheese and smoked salmon. Look for the packets of trimmings which are much cheaper than prime slices.

Preparation time: 10 mins.   *Cooking time: 30 mins.*

2 oz (50g) butter or margarine
¼ pt (150ml) water
2½ oz (65g) plain flour
Pinch salt
2 eggs, beaten

Filling
Smoked salmon trimmings
Cream cheese
Slices cucumber
Slices chicory

1. Pre-heat oven to 220°C (425°F) or Gas No 7.

2. Melt the butter or margarine in a small saucepan, add the water and bring to the boil.

(continued overleaf)

195

3. Stir in the flour and salt all at once and beat over a low heat until the mixture leaves the side of the pan. Allow to cool for a minute or two.

4. Gradually add the eggs, beating well between each addition until the pastry is smooth.

5. Spoon four heaps of the choux pastry on to a damp baking tray and cook for 10 minutes. Turn oven down to 190°C (375°F) or Gas No 5 for a further 15-20 minutes. Allow to cool.

6. Gently pull the buns apart to make an opening and fill with smoked salmon, cream cheese, cucumber and chicory.

AVOCADO AND CORIANDER DIP   *Serves 4*

Crispy fried potato skins, served with a variety of tasty dips, feature frequently on wine bar menus. Port and Stilton, Chilli Meat and Cheddar, Wine and Sweetcorn are all popular but this is one of my favourites.

Preparation time: 10 mins.   *Cooking time: 10 mins.*

2 avocados
2 tablsp garlic mayonnaise
Juice 1 lime
Salt and pepper
2 tablsp chopped fresh coriander
Small (12 oz/340g) can asparagus tips, drained

1. Halve, peel and de-stone the avocados.

2. Mash the flesh in a small bowl.

3. Stir in the mayonnaise, lime juice, seasoning and coriander.

4. Roughly chop the asparagus tips and stir them into the avocado mixture.

5. Divide the mixture between 4 individual dishes.

   Serve the dip with chunks of potato which have been par-boiled for about 5 minutes then fried in hot oil for a further 5 minutes. Drain on kitchen paper. A selection of crudités also makes a good accompaniment.

OMELETTE AUX FINES HERBS *Serves 1*

For a quiet evening alone, after a long, hard day, there is nothing nicer, or quicker, than a light omelette with a golden outside, fluffy and creamy inside and flavoured with chopped fresh herbs from the garden.

Preparation time: 5 mins.   *Cooking time: 5 mins.*

2-3 eggs, depending on size
1 teasp water
Salt and pepper
1 tablsp roughly chopped herbs – chives, parsley,
   tarragon and chervil
Knob butter for frying

1. Beat the eggs, water, seasoning and herbs together, just enough to break down the egg.

2. Melt the butter in an omelette, or small frying pan, and when fairly hot pour in the egg mixture.

3. As the egg begins to set around the edges, use a spatula or spoon to draw the cooked egg into the centre, thus letting uncooked mixture run underneath.

4. When the egg has set, cook for a minute until golden underneath. Fold the omelette in half and serve immediately.

197

14   DESSERTS

Most busy cooks I know hardly ever make sweets during the week, relying instead on yoghurt and fresh fruit. It is of course a good choice. Different combinations of prepared fruit – fresh, dried and canned – make a welcome change from a whole apple or orange so I have included a few ideas.

The more interesting desserts are time-consuming, often expensive and do nothing for figure and health! As a treat though, it is sometimes nice to strike a happy medium between nothing and the elaborate.

Children always seem to suffer from a sweet tooth – and most men too – so hopefully some of these recipes will provide the occasional answer to plaintive cries of 'what's for afters?'

BANANA AND ORANGE FUDGE
Serves 4

This syrupy fruit dessert is delicious on its own but really scrumptious spooned over ice cream. Experiment with different combinations of fruit.

Preparation time: 8 mins.   *Cooking time: 10 mins.*

Small knob of butter or margarine
1 tablsp flaked almonds
1 tablsp soft brown sugar
4 fl oz (100ml) orange juice
2 oranges
2 bananas

1. Melt the butter or margarine and brown the almonds for a couple of minutes.

2. Add the sugar and orange juice and boil until liquid has reduced and begins to caramelise, about 8 minutes.

3. Meanwhile remove the skin and pith from the oranges with a sharp knife. Cut the flesh into bite-size pieces.

4. Peel and slice the bananas.

5. Stir the fruit into the syrup sauce thoroughly.

ORANGE BOODLE

Serves 4

The combination of orange and soured cream results in a light and refreshing dessert. The mixture needs about an hour to set but can be made the day before.

Preparation time: 15 mins.   *Cooking time: None.*

Juice 2 large oranges
5 fl oz (150ml) carton soured cream
2 tablsp soft brown sugar
4 oz (100g) packet sponge fingers
1 small orange for decoration (optional)

1. Mix the orange juice, soured cream and sugar well together.

2. Break the sponge fingers in half and divide between four small glass sundae dishes.

3. Pour the orange and cream mixture over the sponge fingers.

4. Chill for about an hour to set. During this time occasionally press down the sponge fingers.

5. Decorate with a twist of orange if liked.

PINEAPPLE AND MELON PLATTER   *Serves 6-8*

According to research in the USA, pineapples contain rich quantities of the natural enzyme, bromelain, which helps prevent and break up dangerous blood clots. Don't go mad though, one or two pineapples a week are enough!

Preparation time: 20 mins.   *Cooking time: None.*

1 pineapple
1 melon
Icing sugar
Desiccated coconut

1. Cut the top and bottom off the pineapple and stand it upright. Using a sharp knife cut off the thick skin, following the natural curve of the fruit. Cut the flesh into rings and cut out the inner core.

2. Prepare the melon in the same way, removing the seeds.

3. Lay the melon and pineapple rings in a shallow serving dish and sprinkle liberally with icing sugar and desiccated coconut.

PINEAPPLE ROMANOFF   *Serves 4*

This is a simple yet impressive dessert. Strawberries and raspberries can be used in the same way.

Preparation time: 20 mins.   *Cooking time: None.*

1 pineapple
4 tablsp icing sugar
3 tablsp Cointreau
3 tablsp Kirsch

(continued overleaf)

½ pt (300ml) double cream
Thinly pared and shredded orange rind (optional)

1. Remove the skin from the pineapple (see previous recipe). Cut fruit into quarters and remove the core. Cut flesh into bite-size chunks and place in a bowl.

2. Sprinkle on the icing sugar, Cointreau and Kirsch and mix well.

3. Whip cream until it holds its shape then fold through the pineapple mixture. Pile into individual glass dishes and decorate with finely shredded orange rind if liked.

MELON, GRAPE AND GINGER SALAD   *Serves 4-6*

I think the small Charentais melons are ideal for this dish because they have a more distinctive flavour than the other varieties.

Preparation time: 20 mins.   *Cooking time: None.*

2 Charentais melons
Few black and green grapes
Knob fresh ginger, peeled and coarsely grated

1. Cut the melons in half and discard the pips. Scoop out the flesh with a melon baller, or use a spoon and cut into chunks.

2. Halve the grapes and remove the pips. Time and personal preference will dictate whether you peel them.

3. Pile the fruit into individual glass dishes and top with grated ginger.

BLACK CHERRY CRUNCH   *Serves 4*

This is a good way to 'stretch' a can of black cherries.

Preparation time: 20 mins.   *Cooking time: None.*

14 oz (400g) can black cherries
5 fl oz (150ml) carton soured cream
1 tablsp black cherry jam
20 ratafia biscuits

1. De-stone the cherries.

2. Mix the soured cream and jam well together and fold into the cherries.

3. Break or cut each ratafia roughly into four and stir into the cherry mixture. Serve in individual glass dishes.

PEARS IN RED WINE   *Serves 4*

A classic dessert which looks attractive because the wine imparts a rosy hue to the pears. Personal preference will dictate whether to leave the pears whole, which looks more attractive for presentation purposes, or to halve and core them, which is easier to eat.

Preparation time: 10 mins.   *Cooking time: 30 mins.*

4 good quality pears
½ pt (300ml) good full-bodied red wine
1 stick cinnamon
1 whole clove
1 tablsp soft brown sugar

1. If cooking whole pears, peel them leaving the stalks on if

(continued overleaf)

possible. Otherwise halve the pears and remove peel and core.

2. Poach the pears gently in the wine, cinnamon stick and clove for about 20 minutes. Baste and turn several times during cooking.

3. Remove cinnamon stick and clove and discard. Remove pears with a slotted spoon and arrange in a glass serving dish. Add the sugar to the wine and boil until syrupy, about 8 minutes. Pour the sauce over the pears and serve warm or cold with cream.

HONEYED FRUIT KEBABS

Choose a selection of fresh or canned exotic fruit and allow one long skewer or two shorter ones per person. If liked, the prepared fruit can be marinaded overnight in a liqueur.

Preparation time: 10-15 mins. *Cooking time: 8 mins.*

Chunks of fresh pineapple
Whole apricots
Lychees
Black grapes
Bananas, cut in four
Halved and peeled peaches
Clear honey

1. Prepare the fruit, thread on skewers and spoon a little clear honey over.

2. Cook under a very hot grill, about 4 minutes either side, until the honey caramelises.

ICE CREAM WITH HOT CHOCOLATE SAUCE

Serves 4

Ice cream provides a good base for a number of emergency desserts. The melba sauce in the Peach Melba recipe also goes well on ice cream.

Preparation time: 5 mins.   *Cooking time: 8 mins.*

2 oz (50g) plain chocolate
Knob butter or margarine
1 tablsp milk
1 teasp vanilla essence
4 scoops of vanilla ice cream

1. Put the chocolate and butter or margarine in a small bowl and stand it in a pan of hot water on the stove to melt.

2. Stir in the milk and vanilla essence to make a smooth creamy sauce. Do not overheat.

3. Place a scoop of ice cream in individual sundae dishes and pour over the warm sauce.

BUTTERSCOTCH SAUCE

This is another old favourite which is quickly made from stock ingredients.

Preparation time: 5 mins.   *Cooking time: 5 mins.*

2 oz (50g) butter or margarine
4 tablsp soft brown sugar
2 tablsp golden syrup

1. Put all three ingredients in a small saucepan and heat gently until smooth and well blended.

(continued overleaf)

2. Boil for about 5 minutes until the mixture begins to thicken. Serve over vanilla ice cream.

PEACH MELBA   *Serves 4*

If possible use fresh peaches as they are much nicer. Out of season or in an emergency, use canned peach halves.

Preparation time: 8 mins.   *Cooking time: 10 mins.*

¼ pt (150ml) water
2 oz (50g) granulated sugar
4 tablsp raspberry jam
Juice ½ lemon
Few drops almond essence (optional)
4 scoops vanilla ice cream
2 fresh peaches, halved (and skinned if liked)

1. Put the water and sugar in a small saucepan and heat gently until the sugar has dissolved.

2. Boil rapidly for about 5 minutes until the liquid has thickened and reduced slightly.

3. Remove from heat and stir in the jam, lemon juice and almond essence.

4. Heat gently, stirring all the time until the ingredients are well blended. The sauce should just coat the back of the spoon. If it is too thin, boil for a further couple of minutes.

5. Place a scoop of ice cream in 4 sundae dishes, top with a peach half and pour over the melba sauce.

APRICOT MOUSSE

As long as you have a liquidiser this is quick and simple to make yet delicious to eat. The mousse needs time to set so is best made the night before.

Preparation time: 15 mins.   *Cooking time: None.*

½ oz (12.5g) packet gelatine
2 tablsp apricot juice
14 oz (397g) can apricots
½ oz (12.5g) sugar
Squeeze lemon juice
5 fl oz (150ml) carton double cream
Whipped double cream for decoration (optional)

1. Put the gelatine and 2 tablespoons of the apricot juice in a small bowl and stand it in a pan of hot water to dissolve.

2. Drain the apricots and liquidise all but one.

3. Add the dissolved gelatine, sugar, lemon juice and cream and liquidise for a couple of minutes.

4. Pour into 4 individual dishes and chill until set.

5. Decorate each with a piece of apricot and some piped whipped cream if liked.

FRUIT PASTRIES

This, and the following recipe, are easily made yet look as though you have spent hours creating French pâtisserie! To save further time, cook the vol-au-vents and puff pastry the night before. For special occasions, pipe a swirl of cream on top of the fromage frais before decorating with fruit.

Preparation time: 15 mins.   *Cooking time: 12 mins.*

8 small frozen vol-au-vents
2 oz (50g) plain chocolate
2 × 4 oz (100g) pots fruit-flavoured fromage frais
8 fresh strawberries or 1 kiwi fruit
Whipped cream for decoration (optional)

1. Pre-heat oven to 220°C (425°F) or Gas No 7.

2. Cook the vol-au-vents for about 12 minutes until well risen and lightly brown. Allow to cool.

3. Meanwhile put the chocolate in a small bowl and stand it in a pan of hot water on the stove to melt. Do not overheat.

4. Discard the lids and pull out any uncooked pastry from the vol-au-vents.

5. Dip the tops of the vol-au-vents in the melted chocolate and arrange on a serving plate.

6. Using a teaspoon, carefully fill the vol-au-vents with fromage frais.

7. Top with a swirl of whipped cream if liked, and a fresh strawberry or slice of kiwi fruit.

Another version of the above can be made by filling cooked vol-au-vents with canned custard, to which 2 teaspoons of vanilla essence and a little whipped cream have been added. Pop a strawberry or slice of fresh peach on top and dust all over with sieved icing sugar.

PINEAPPLE GALETTE

Serves 4-6

This delicious dessert can be made as plain or as fancy as you like. For a special occasion, add a touch of luxury by including all the optional ingredients. For an economical family dessert simply leave them out. Save further time by buying individual squares of frozen puff pastry – no rolling out and no cutting to size. If possible, cook the pastry the night before.

Preparation time: 15 mins.   *Cooking time: 10 mins.*

3 squares frozen puff pastry
15 oz (425g) can crushed pineapple
2 teasp Kirsch or other liqueur (optional)
5 fl oz (150ml) carton double cream (optional)
15 oz (425g) can custard
3 teasp vanilla essence (optional)
4 tablsp icing sugar (optional)
Toasted flaked almonds (optional)

1. Pre-heat oven to 220°C (425°F) or Gas No 7.

2. Lay the sheets of pastry on a baking tray and prick all over with a fork. Cook for about 10 minutes until well risen and lightly brown. Allow to cool.

3. Meanwhile, drain the pineapple, reserving the juice, and stir the liqueur into the flesh.

4. Whip the cream until it just holds its shape.

5. Stir the cream into the custard, together with the vanilla essence.

6. Cut each pastry slice into two horizontally and flatten all but one half (which will be the top) gently with the palm of your hand.

7. Sandwich together the pastry sheets, pineapple and custard

(continued overleaf)

209

mixture in alternate layers, ending with the top piece of pastry.

8. Make up a thick glacé icing with the icing sugar and a little pineapple juice. Drizzle over the top of the galette. (If time is short, simply dust the top with caster sugar.)

9. Sprinkle toasted flaked almonds over the icing.

N.B. The recipe is designed for generous amounts of custard between the layers. If you feel there is too much, serve any excess separately.

APPLE CREAM BRÛLÉE   *Serves 4*

Caramelised sugar gives a crunchy, sweet topping which contrasts well with the sharp tang of apple on a thick cream base. Serve with Continental-style biscuits.

Preparation time: 10 mins.   *Cooking time: 10 mins.*

5 fl oz (150ml) carton double cream
8 oz (225g) carton Greek yoghurt
2 teasp vanilla essence
1 large OR 2 small crisp eating apples
Juice ½ lemon
1 teasp powdered ginger
4 tablsp demerara sugar

1. Whip the cream until it holds its shape then mix in the yoghurt and vanilla essence.

2. Pour the cream mixture into a shallow ovenproof dish.

3. Cut the apples into quarters, discard core and thinly slice the flesh.

4. Arrange the apple on top of the cream mixture and sprinkle on the lemon juice and ginger.

5. Spoon over the sugar and cook under a medium grill for about 10 minutes, until the sugar has caramelised. Serve hot or cold.

DATE AND HONEY CREAM

Serves 4

Honey acts as a natural sweetener in this recipe, and by combining the cream with yoghurt a certain amount of richness is eliminated. For quickness buy ready chopped dates.

Preparation time: 5 mins.   *Cooking time: None.*

5 fl oz (150ml) double cream
8 oz (225g) carton Greek yoghurt
4 oz (100g) chopped dates
Clear honey

1. Whip cream until it just holds its shape.

2. Stir in the yoghurt and dates.

3. Divide the mixture between 4 glass dishes and trickle a little honey over each.

STRAWBERRY RING

Serves 4-6

Choux pastry is made easily and quickly with store cupboard ingredients and is ideal for entertaining in a hurry. If fresh strawberries are not available, use canned peach slices or black cherries. The pastry won't spoil if made the night before.

Preparation time: 15 mins.   *Cooking time: 30 mins.*

2 oz (50g) butter or margarine
¼ pt (150ml) water
2½ oz (65g) plain flour

(continued overleaf)

Pinch salt
2 eggs, beaten

Filling
½ pt (300ml) carton double cream, whipped
Fresh strawberries or fruit of choice
Icing sugar

1. Pre-heat oven to 220°C (425°F) or Gas No 7.

2. Melt the butter or margarine in a small saucepan, add the water and bring to the boil.

3. Stir in the flour and salt all at once and beat over a low heat until the mixture leaves the side of the pan. Allow to cool for a minute or two.

4. Gradually beat in the eggs, beating well between each addition until the pastry is smooth.

5. Put dessertspoonfuls of mixture in a circle on a damp baking tray, making sure each spoonful touches the other.

6. Bake in the oven for 10 minutes, then turn down to 190°C (375°F) or Gas No 5 and bake for a further 20 minutes. Allow to cool.

7. Split the pastry ring in two horizontally and sandwich together with whipped cream and sliced strawberries. Dust the top with sieved icing sugar.

PINEAPPLE UPSIDE-DOWN CAKE

Serves 4

Golden syrup and pineapple combine to make a delicious gooey base to a standard sponge mixture.

Preparation time: 10 mins.   *Cooking time: 25 mins.*

4 tablsp golden syrup
8 oz (225g) pineapple rings
4 oz (100g) margarine
4 oz (100g) caster sugar
2 size 2 eggs, beaten
4 oz (100g) self-raising flour

1. Pre-heat oven to 180°C (350°F) or Gas No 4.

2. Grease and flour an 8" (20.5cm) sandwich tin.

3. Put the syrup and 1 tablespoon of the pineapple juice in the base of the sandwich tin and lay the pineapple rings on top.

4. Cream the margarine and sugar together until light and fluffy.

5. Gradually add the eggs, beating well between each addition.

6. Fold the sieved flour into the mixture and spoon on top of the pineapple.

7. Bake for about 20-25 minutes until the sponge is lightly brown and firm to the touch. Turn the cake out of the tin upside-down, and serve.

SYRUP TART   *Serves 4*

An old favourite which children usually can't get enough of.

Preparation time: 15 mins.   *Cooking time: 20 mins.*

8 oz (225g) short crust pastry (see page 234 or use frozen, defrosted)
6 tablsp golden syrup
2 oz (50g) fresh white breadcrumbs

1. Pre-heat oven to 200°C (400°F) or Gas No 6.

2. Make the pastry as per page 234 (or take the defrosted frozen pastry) and use it to line a 7-8" (18-20.5cm) flan ring or sandwich tin.

3. Spoon the syrup into the pastry case and sprinkle the breadcrumbs on top.

4. Bake for about 20 minutes.

BLACKBERRY JELLY

This is a particularly nice way of serving blackberries and encourages children to eat fresh fruit.

Preparation time: 10 mins.   *Cooking time: None.*

1 tablet raspberry or blackcurrant jelly
8 oz (225g) blackberries

1. Make up the jelly according to manufacturer's instructions.
2. Chill until quite cold and then stir in the blackberries and leave until completely set.

Tip: other economical desserts can be made with virtually any fruit in season. Try diced apple and pear in lemon jelly or orange segments in orange jelly.

15 CAKES

When it comes to quality there is nothing quite like a home-made cake. A couple of slices are a good wholesome fill-me-up for hungry children when they come home from school. Cake also makes a good standby for an after-supper dessert.

Although cake-making is a fascinating art, it is not difficult. All are made with a few simple ingredients and if you have flour, margarine, sugar, eggs and some dried fruit in stock, you can always make a cake!

The following examples are designed to be easy on your time and easy on your pocket too.

To test if a cake is cooked, run a thin skewer into the centre. If it comes out clean the cake is cooked but, if any uncooked mixture is adhering to the skewer, leave the cake in the oven for a little longer. If the outside is looking too dark, turn the oven down a fraction.

DATE AND WALNUT LOAF

Nothing could be simpler to make than this delicious cake. No arm-aching mixing, whisking or beating either!

Preparation time: 8 mins.   *Cooking time: 50 mins.*

6 oz (175g) chopped dates
3 oz (75g) walnut pieces
4 oz (100g) demerara sugar
2 oz (50g) margarine
¼ pt (150ml) boiling water
1 size 2 egg, beaten
8 oz (225g) self-raising flour

1. Pre-heat oven to 180°C (350°F) or Gas No 4.

2. Grease and flour a medium sized loaf tin.

3. Put the dates, nuts, sugar and margarine in a bowl and mix in the boiling water. Stir until the margarine has melted.

4. Stir in the beaten egg and then fold in the sieved flour.

5. Pour mixture into the loaf tin and bake for 45-50 minutes.

VAL'S TEA BREAD

Measure ingredients in a standard size cup throughout for perfect results. Use whatever dried fruit is in the cupboard – sultanas, seedless raisins or currants, or a mixture of all three.

Preparation time: 5 mins + overnight soaking

Cooking time: 1 hour

1 lb (450g) dried fruit
1 cup black tea
1 cup demerara sugar
1 size 2 egg, beaten
1 cup self-raising flour

1.   Soak the dried fruit, tea and sugar in a bowl overnight.

2.   Pre-heat oven to 150°C (300°F) or Gas No 2.

3.   Grease and flour a medium size loaf tin.

4.   Stir the egg into the fruit mixture and then fold in the sieved flour.

5.   Pour into the tin and bake for about 1 hour.

BRAN AND APRICOT LOAF

Use the same standard size teacup throughout. The loaf is delicious sliced and buttered. If preferred, sultanas can be used instead of apricots.

Preparation time: 5 mins. + 1 hour soaking time
Cooking time: 40 mins.

1 cup bran
1 cup soft brown sugar
4 oz (100g) dried apricots, snipped into small pieces
1 tablsp golden syrup
1 cup milk, warmed
1 cup self-raising flour

1. Put the bran, sugar, apricots, syrup and warm milk into a bowl, mix well and leave to stand for 1 hour.

2. Pre-heat oven to 180°C (350°F) or Gas No 4.

3. Grease and flour a small or medium sized loaf tin.

4. Fold the sieved flour into the bran mixture, put into the tin and bake for about 40 minutes. Turn out and cool on a wire rack.

GENOESE SPONGE

This is a super-light sponge mixture which forms the basis of fruit gâteaux. It is ideal for a special occasion dessert or a teatime treat when filled with jam and cream.

Preparation time: 25 mins.   *Cooking time: 15 mins.*

3 oz (75g) margarine
3 size 2 eggs
4 oz (100g) caster sugar
3 oz (75g) self-raising flour

1. Pre-heat oven to 180°C (350°F) or Gas No 4.

2. Melt the margarine in a small saucepan in a microwave.

3. Put the eggs and sugar in a large bowl and stand it over a saucepan of hot water.

4. Whisk the eggs and sugar until the mixture is light in colour and thick enough to retain the impression of the whisk, about 20 minutes.

5. Grease and flour two 7" (18cm) sandwich tins.

6. Fold the sieved flour and melted margarine, a little at a time, into the whisked mixture until they are all used up. (The mixture must be very lightly mixed or volume will be lost, resulting in a flat, heavy cake.)

7. Pour the mixture into the prepared tins and bake for about 15 minutes until golden brown and springy to the touch.

8. Turn out on to a wire rack to cool.

Tip: For a special occasion dessert, split each sponge into two and then layer back together with fruit and whipped cream. Fresh raspberries or strawberries are particularly delicious. Dust the top with sieved icing sugar. A more economical version can be made using chopped canned peaches.

FLAPJACKS

Makes about 16

An easily made and nutritious chewy treat.

Preparation time: 10 mins.   *Cooking time: 20 mins.*

4 oz (100g) margarine
4 oz (100g) demerara OR soft brown sugar
3 tablsp golden syrup
8 oz (225g) porridge oats

1. Melt the margarine, sugar and syrup in a saucepan.

2. Meanwhile, heat oven to 180°C (350°F) or Gas No 4.

3. Grease an 8" (20.5cm) square tin.

4. Stir the oats into the syrup mixture and mix well.

5. Turn into the greased tin, press down and bake for about 20 minutes.

6. Mark into squares when hot and remove from tin when cold.

TRADITIONAL SHORTBREAD

Shortbread is always popular and if you plan to make a lot, it is worth investing a few pounds in a traditional mould. These are available from specialist kitchen shops and produce an attractive and professional result.

Preparation time: 20 mins.   *Cooking time: 25 mins.*

3 oz (75g) butter (straight from fridge)
2 oz (50g) icing sugar, sieved
4 oz (100g) plain flour, sieved
Icing sugar to finish

1. Pre-heat oven to 170°C (325°F) or Gas No 3.

2. Put the butter and icing sugar on a work surface and knead together until all the sugar has been absorbed.

3. Gradually knead in the flour until a smooth softish dough is formed.

4. Press the dough into a greased 7" (18cm) sandwich tin or special shortbread mould, and bake for about 25 minutes until golden brown. Turn out when cool and dust with icing sugar.

16 BACK TO BASICS

This section offers ideas for suitable accompaniments to everyday meals. Basic recipes are also given for items like pastry, sauces and batters which crop up several times throughout the book. All are easily made at home at a fraction of the cost that you would expect to pay for commercially prepared equivalents.

Short crust pastry, dumplings, pancakes and basic sauces are a cheap way of making a more substantial meal out of bits and pieces and 'stretching' more expensive ingredients like meat, fish and fruit.

Short crust pastry is used for pies, flans and quiches; dumplings can be popped into soups and casseroles; and pancakes are delicious with a variety of sweet and savoury fillings. Using a packet white sauce is three times dearer than home-made and, contrary to popular belief, isn't any quicker. Try my one-stage method on page 249 and prove it! Basic white sauce can be flavoured with chopped cooked onion, chopped parsley or grated cheese to bring variety to the weekly menu.

Ready-made potato dishes cost a fortune. Frozen chips, instant mash, potato salad and hash browns can cost up to four times as much as making your own.

BREAD

If someone had told me that one day I'd be baking my own bread I would have roared with laughter. For bread-making is time-consuming and fiddly, is it not, and therefore not worth the hassle? Yet it only takes 15-20 minutes to make the dough and the only ingredients needed are flour, yeast, salt, sugar and water. The lengthy bit is leaving the dough to rise (known as proving) but you can always do something else in the meantime. Try making a batch one wet Sunday afternoon; even better, get the kids pummelling away at the dough while you put your feet up!

Home-made bread is best eaten within a day of baking, but it will keep in reasonable condition for two to three days when stored in a tightly sealed polythene bag. After that time, thick slices make excellent Garlic Bread (see page 227). Alternatively, make breadcrumbs which are useful for coating food prior to frying or for giving crunchy toppings to a variety of savoury dishes. Store the breadcrumbs in a lidded jar in the fridge until ready to use.

Tips For Successful Bread-Making

Strong white bread flour absorbs more water than ordinary flour because it has a higher gluten content. This results in a bigger loaf and lighter texture.

Wholemeal bread won't rise so much as a white loaf because the wholemeal flour contains less gluten than white. This prevents the yeast working quite so well.

If the water used for mixing the dough is too hot, the yeast will be killed and the bread will fail to rise. Water should therefore be luke-warm; dip your little finger into the measuring jug, the water should feel neither hot nor cold.

For the same reason, avoid leaving the dough to rise in too hot a spot. An airing cupboard or near a radiator is an ideal place.

Save time by using easy-blend dried yeast. This is available from supermarkets in boxes of eight sachets and, unlike fresh yeast or ordinary dried yeast, it can be sprinkled directly on to the flour which speeds up preparation.

Save further time by freezing uncooked dough. Make several batches in one go and then bake each loaf as you need it. Stored in an oiled, polythene bag, uncooked bread dough can be frozen for up to 3 months. Frozen dough should be thawed and then left to rise as usual before baking.

Two recipes are given here: one for basic white bread and one for wholemeal bread. If you like, you can use a combination of flours. Speciality breads can be made by adding flavourings like dried or freshly chopped herbs, finely chopped garlic or grated cheese. Or press a few black olives into the top of the dough before leaving it to rise.

What Went Wrong?
The most common mistake in bread-making is lack of patience!

If the baked bread is dense in texture, either the dough was insufficiently kneaded or not left to rise long enough.

If, on the other hand, the dough is left to rise for too long, it can collapse which results in wet and heavy bread. Generally speaking, the dough should reach the top of the tin prior to baking.

If at first you don't succeed, try again! Eventually you are bound to produce professional-looking bread. And remember, there is nothing quite like a chunk of home-made crusty bread to accompany soups, salads and many vegetarian dishes.

Tip:
Where reference is made in the recipes to a 1 lb (450g) loaf tin, the approximate size is 8" × 4" (20.5cm × 10cm); and a 2 lb (900g) tin is about 9" × 5" (23cm × 13cm).

QUICK WHITE BREAD

(makes 1 large loaf or 2 small)

Preparation time: 15 mins.   *Cooking time: 20-40 mins.*

1 lb 6 oz (625g) strong white flour
1 level teasp salt
1 rounded teasp sugar
1 sachet easy-blend dried yeast
¾ pt (425ml) luke-warm water

1. Sieve the flour into a large bowl.

2. Mix in the salt and sugar.

3. Sprinkle on the yeast.

4. Pour on the warm water and mix to an elastic dough using a round-bladed knife.

5. Turn the dough on to a floured surface and knead for 10 minutes.

6. Grease and flour one 2 lb (900g) or two 1 lb (450g) tin(s), add the dough, and cover with greaseproof paper.

7. Leave in a warm place for about 30-40 minutes until the dough has doubled in size or reached the top of the tin.

8. Pre-heat oven to 200°C (400°F) or Gas No 6.

9. Remove the covering paper before baking.

10. Bake large loaves for about 30-40 minutes and small loaves for about 20 minutes.

11. Remove from tin and leave on a wire rack to cool.

Tip: If the bread has been baked long enough it should sound hollow when tapped on the bottom. If you feel the bread is not quite cooked, pop it back in the oven without the tin.

QUICK WHOLEMEAL BREAD

(makes 1 large loaf or 2 small)

Wholemeal bread has more flavour than white, keeps better and is a valuable source of dietary fibre.

Preparation time: 15 mins.   *Cooking time: 20-40 mins.*

1½ lb (700g) plain wholemeal flour
1 level teasp sugar
1 sachet easy-blend dried yeast
¾ pt (425ml) luke-warm water

Follow instructions in the previous recipe for making and cooking but do not sieve the wholemeal flour.

GARLIC BREAD

This is a good way of using up semi-stale bread or your first attempts which may not have turned out quite right!

Simply butter 4 thick slices of white or wholemeal bread and then spread on some finely chopped garlic. Place the slices on a baking tray and cook for 6-10 minutes in a hot oven, 200°C (400°F) or Gas No 6.

PIZZA

Commercially prepared pizzas cost a fortune and they're not always overly generous on taste and abundance of topping. You can put almost anything you like on a home-made version so take the following recipe as an idea only. It happens to be my particular favourite! According to personal preference choose from ham, pineapple, onions, mushrooms, peppers, chillies, bacon, salami, tuna fish, olives, spring onions, anchovies and garlic. The only two essential ingredients, which form the basis of all pizzas, are tomatoes and cheese. In fact, if you're really pushed for money, a tasty pizza can be made from using these alone.

Pizza base is the same as a bread dough (see page 226). White or wholemeal flour can be used or strong white or bread flour.

The only accompaniment necessary is a nice mixed salad, tossed in a vinaigrette dressing.

*Tip:*Mozzarella cheese – the type that goes all gooey and stringy when cooked – is traditionally used for pizzas. As this is expensive, I mix it with grated Cheddar because the secret of a good pizza is to have a generous topping of golden bubbly cheese.

BASIC PIZZA DOUGH
Serves 4

This quantity makes about 10-12" (25.5-30.5cm) pizzas or four individual pizzas of about 7½" (19cm) each.

Preparation time: 15 mins. + 30 mins. for the dough to rise

1 lb (450g) plain white or wholemeal flour
1 level teasp sugar
1 level teasp salt
1 sachet easy-blend dried yeast
½ pt (300ml) luke warm water

1. Put the flour, sugar and salt together in a bowl and mix in the easy-blend dried yeast.

2. Using a round-bladed knife, stir in the water to form an elastic dough.

3. Turn the dough on to a floured surface and knead for 10 minutes.

4. Cut the dough into either 2 or 4 pieces and roll each out into rounds about ⅜" (1cm) thick.

5. Lay the pizza bases on an oiled baking tray and put in a warm place for about 30 minutes until the dough is puffy.

MY FAVOURITE PIZZA

Serves 4

Preparation time: 10 mins. + making the dough

Cooking time: 20 mins.

1 lb (450g) pizza dough (see previous recipe)
1 oz (25g) margarine
4 oz (100g) mushrooms, sliced
3-4 tablsp tomato purée
14 oz (397g) can peeled tomatoes, drained
Salt and freshly ground black pepper
1 tablsp chopped fresh basil (optional)
3-4 spring onions, chopped
4 oz (100g) sliced spicy sausage or salami
6 oz (175g) Mozzarella cheese, grated
2 oz (50g) tasty Cheddar cheese, grated

1. Make the pizza bases and leave to rise as per the previous recipe.

2. Meanwhile, melt the margarine and sauté the mushrooms for 5 minutes.

3. When the pizza bases have risen slightly and become puffy, press the dough down gently to within 1" (2.5cm) of the edge.

4. Pre-heat the oven to 200°C (400°F) or Gas No 6.

5. Spread the pizza bases with tomato purée to within 1" (2.5cm) of the edge.

6. Top with a layer of sliced canned tomatoes.

7. Sprinkle with salt, pepper, basil and spring onions.

8. Spread on a layer of mushrooms and top with sliced spicy sausage or salami.

9. Mix the two cheeses together and sprinkle on top of the pizzas.

10. Bake for about 15-20 minutes until the pizza crust is golden and the cheese brown and bubbly.

BARGAIN PIZZA

Serves 4

Preparation time: 10 mins + making the dough
Cooking time: 20 mins.

1 lb (450g) pizza dough (see page 229)
4 tablsp tomato purée
14 oz (397g) can peeled tomatoes, drained
Salt and freshly ground black pepper
1 tablsp chopped fresh basil (optional)
6 oz (175g) Mozzarella cheese, grated
2 oz (50g) tasty Cheddar cheese, grated

1. Make the pizza bases and leave to rise according to instructions on page 229.

2. Pre-heat oven to 200°C (400°F) or Gas No 6.

3. When the pizza bases have risen slightly and become puffy, press the dough down gently to within 1" (2.5cm) of the edge.

4. Spread with tomato purée and top with sliced canned tomatoes. Sprinkle with salt, pepper and basil.

5. Mix the cheeses together and sprinkle on top of the pizzas.

6. Bake for 15-20 minutes until golden and bubbly.

DUMPLINGS

Dumplings are a good way of 'stretching' expensive ingredients like meat, and also for making vegetable casseroles and soups into a more substantial meal. Traditionally beef suet was used but a vegetable version is now produced. Both are available in packets ready shredded. Dumplings are made with white or wholemeal flour and with or without suet.

SUET DUMPLINGS   *Makes about 8-10*

Preparation time: 10 mins.   *Cooking time: 15-20 mins.*

4 oz (100g) white self-raising flour
½ level teasp salt
2 oz (50g) shredded beef or vegetable suet
Little cold water

1. Sieve the flour and salt into a bowl, then stir in the suet.

2. Using a round-bladed knife, mix to an elastic consistency with a little cold water.

3. Form into small balls and add to soups or casseroles 15-20 minutes before the end of the cooking time.

HERB DUMPLINGS (without suet) *Makes about 8-10*

Preparation time: 10 mins.   *Cooking time: 15-20 mins.*

4 oz (100g) self-raising wholemeal flour
½ level teasp salt
1 oz (25g) margarine
1 teasp dried mixed herbs OR 1 tablsp fresh chopped
   herbs
Freshly ground black pepper
1 size 3 egg, beaten
Little milk

1. Sieve the flour and salt into a bowl.

2. Rub in the margarine until the mixture resembles fine breadcrumbs.

3. Stir in the mixed herbs and a little pepper.

4. Using a round-bladed knife, stir in the egg and a little milk to give an elastic consistency.

5. Form into small balls and add to soups or casseroles 15-20 minutes before the end of the cooking time.

PASTRY

Short crust pastry is used for sweet and savoury pies, flans, quiches and pasties. Pastry adds bulk, making a tasty meal from a little filling.

It can be made with white or wholemeal flour, or half of each. Wholemeal pastry is more grainy than that made with white flour and has more of a tendency to crumble when being rolled out. Nonetheless many people prefer its crunchier texture and wholesome food value.

Block margarine works best as it is harder and colder and can easily be cut into correct measurements without the need for weighing, and it is cheaper than soft margarine! The rule is half fat to flour, so if you need 4 oz (100g) pastry simply halve the ingredients in the following recipes.

For best results handle pastry as little as possible and keep ingredients cold. Only use the tips of your fingers when rubbing the fat into the flour. Avoid stretching the pastry when lining a flan ring or covering a pie, for it will shrink back during baking and spoil the finished shape. Add the water cautiously, using just enough to make a stiff dough and roll the pastry as lightly as possible.

Finally, cooked pastry is less likely to be soggy if baked in a metal dish rather than ovenproof china or glass. The exception is when a pie consists of a top crust only.

SHORT CRUST PASTRY

8 oz (225g) plain white flour
¼ level teasp salt
4 oz (100g) margarine
Little cold water

1. Sieve the flour and salt into a bowl.

2. Using the tips of your fingers, rub the margarine into the flour until the mixture resembles fine breadcrumbs.

3. Using a round-bladed knife, mix in a little cold water until a stiff dough is formed.

4. Turn out onto a lightly floured surface, roll out and use as instructed in a particular recipe.

Tip: Wrapped in foil or a polythene bag, excess pastry will keep in the fridge for 2-3 days, or, stored in a polythene bag, it can be frozen for up to 3 months.

Tip: To save time, make large quantities of rubbed-in mixture and freeze in bags for instant pastry mix.

WHOLEMEAL PASTRY

8 oz (225g) plain wholemeal flour
¼ level teasp salt
4 oz (100g) margarine
Little cold water

1. Put the flour and salt into a bowl.

2. Using the tips of your fingers, rub in the margarine until the mixture resembles fine breadcrumbs.

3. Using a round-bladed knife, mix to a stiff dough with a little cold water.

4. Turn on to a floured surface and roll out as required.

Tip: Lining a flan tin with pastry is made easier if you roll the pastry around the rolling pin and then unroll it over the tin. If it breaks, don't panic! Doing a patching job is perfectly acceptable and after all, once the filling is in, only the edges of the pastry show anyway!

BATTERS

Batter makes a versatile base for a wide variety of sweet and savoury meals including pancakes, Yorkshire pudding, toad-in-the-hole and fritters. White or wholemeal flour can be used, depending on personal taste.

PANCAKE BATTER   *(Makes between 8-10 pancakes)*

4 oz (100g) plain white flour
¼ level teasp salt
1 size 3 egg
½ pt (300ml) milk

1. Sieve the flour and salt into a bowl.

2. Make a well in the centre, crack the egg and add a little of the milk.

3. Using the wooden spoon, stir briskly, gradually drawing the flour in from the sides.

4. As the mixture thickens, add more milk until it is all used up, beating well all the time. If time permits leave the batter to stand for 30 minutes before using.

WHOLEMEAL PANCAKE BATTER

Make in the same way as the previous recipe but use 4 oz (100g) plain wholemeal flour instead of white flour.

FRITTER BATTER

This is used as a coating for sweet and savoury fritters and needs to be of a thicker consistency than pancake batter. The addition of bicarbonate of soda results in a nice crispy batter.

4 oz (100g) plain white flour
¼ level teasp salt
1 rounded teasp bicarbonate of soda
1 size 3 egg
¼ pt (150ml) milk

1. Sieve the flour, salt and bicarbonate of soda into a bowl.

2. Make a well in the centre, crack in the egg and add a little of the milk.

3. Stir briskly, gradually adding the rest of the milk, beating well all the time.

POTATOES

Potatoes are an inexpensive source of carbohydrate, protein, iron, calcium, dietary fibre and particularly vitamin C. However, their goodness is easily destroyed and much depends on how they are cooked.

Boil potatoes in small amounts of liquid and drain as soon as they are cooked because vitamin C dissolves in water. A squeeze of lemon juice added to the water when boiling potatoes prevents after-cooking discolouration. Rather than slinging the goodness into the sink, use the liquid in soups and stews.

Even better, bake potatoes in their jackets or cook potatoes in ways where the liquid is part of the dish, e.g. Scalloped Potatoes (page 240) and Bombay Potatoes (page 244).

Cooking potatoes in a microwave retains more vitamin C.

Peel potatoes thinly as the nutrients lie just under the skin. Prepare potatoes just before cooking to preserve these nutrients.

When calculating quantities, allow between 6-8 oz (175-225g) of potatoes per person.

Home-grown potatoes fall roughly into three seasonal groups. In June and July come the earlies, commonly referred to as new potatoes. These are high in fibre and low in fat and are delicious boiled in their skins or used in salads. August through to March sees the second earlies, while September to May produces the main crop.

It is useful to become familiar with certain varieties until you find a particular favourite. For example, some people like a floury-textured jacket potato whereas others may prefer a waxy, firmer flesh.

Desirée: Light yellow flesh and firm texture. Can be roasted, chipped and baked.

Maris Piper: Cream flesh with floury texture. Excellent for boiling, baking, roasting and chipping.

Pentland Squire: White flesh and floury texture. Use for mashing, baking, roasting and chipping.

King Edward: Cream flesh with floury texture. A good all purpose potato but recommended for delicious mash.

Romano: Cream flesh and waxy texture. Good for baking, roasting, boiling and chipping.

BAKED POTATOES

What costs pounds in a wine bar can be made at home for pence! Baking potatoes in their jackets is one of the most wholesome ways of cooking this humble vegetable.

1. Pre-heat oven to 200°C (400°F) or Gas No 6.

2. Scrub the potatoes well, place them on a baking tray and cook for 45 minutes – 1 hour, depending on size.

One of the nicest ways of serving jacket potatoes is with a chunk of butter or margarine and some freshly ground black pepper. For a meal in itself, simply make a cut along the length of the cooked potato, gently squeeze the ends to open it up and then stuff with one of the following fillings:

Soured cream mixed with crisply fried chopped bacon.

Cream cheese mixed with chopped chives.

Flaked tuna fish and sweetcorn bound with mayonnaise.

Any minced beef filling, like left-over Bolognese sauce or cottage pie mixture.

SCALLOPED POTATOES

Serves 4

Preparation time: 15 mins.   *Cooking time: 1 hour*

1½ lb (700g) potatoes
2 oz (50g) margarine
Salt and freshly ground black pepper
12 fl oz (350ml) milk

1. Pre-heat oven to 180°C (350°F) or Gas No 4.

2. Peel and thinly slice the potatoes.

3. Grease a deep ovenproof dish and layer with the sliced potato, dotted with margarine and sprinkled with salt and pepper.

4. Pour the milk into the dish and bake for about 1 hour until the potatoes are tender.

5. Leave to stand for 5 minutes before serving.

Tip: Use large potatoes when making dishes of this kind; not only is it cheaper because there's less waste but also less time is spent peeling.

CHEESY NEW POTATO BAKE *Serves 4*

Serve as an accompaniment to cold meat, chicken drumsticks or quiche, or as a meal on its own with mixed salad and crusty bread.

Preparation time: 10 mins. *Cooking time: 1 hour*

1¼ lb (575g) new potatoes
1 oz (25g) butter or margarine
1 teasp mixed dried herbs OR 1 tablsp chopped fresh
** herbs**
Salt and freshly ground black pepper
2 oz (50g) mature Cheddar cheese, grated

1. Pre-heat oven to 200°C (400°F) or Gas No 6.

2. Grease four squares of foil about 12" (30.5cm) in size.

3. Scrub and slice the potatoes and divide between the pieces of foil.

4. Sprinkle some herbs on each; season with salt and pepper and fold up into parcels.

5. Bake for 40 minutes and then unwrap and top with grated cheese. Bake uncovered for a further 10 minutes until the cheese is golden and bubbly.

ROASTIES

Serves 4

Perfect roast potatoes should be brown and crunchy on the outside and soft and floury inside. Here's how to achieve them!

Preparation time: 15 mins. *Cooking time: 30-40 mins.*

4 oz (100g) lard or dripping
1½ lb (700g) potatoes, peeled

1. Heat the fat in a roasting tin in a hot oven (220°C/425°F or Gas No 7).

2. Cook the potatoes in boiling, salted water for 6-10 minutes, depending on size. (This is known as par-boiling.) Drain well.

3. Return the potatoes to the pan and give them a good shake to fluff up the edges.

4. Transfer the potatoes to the roasting tin and spoon over the hot fat.

5. Bake for about 30-40 minutes, turning the potatoes occasionally. Drain on kitchen paper.

HASH BROWNS

Serves 4

Preparation time: 15 mins.   *Cooking time: 30 mins.*

2 lb (900g) potatoes, peeled
2 tablsp oil
1 oz (25g) butter or margarine
Salt and freshly ground black pepper

1. Par-boil the potatoes (see page 29) for 7-10 minutes, depending on size. Drain and allow to cool.

2. Heat the oil and butter or margarine in a large frying pan.

3. Coarsely grate the potatoes straight into the pan and season with salt and pepper.

4. Using a spatula or fish slice, press the potato into a round and fry gently for 15 minutes.

5. Turn the potato over and fry the other side until brown.

BOMBAY POTATOES

Serve these tasty potatoes on their own with fresh crusty bread or as an accompaniment to cold meat or sausages.

Preparation time: 15 mins.   *Cooking time: 50 mins.*

1½ lb (700g) potatoes, peeled and diced
4 tablsp oil
2 level teasp mustard seeds
2 level teasp cumin
1 level teasp coriander
1 level teasp turmeric
1 large onion, peeled and chopped
2 cloves garlic, peeled and finely chopped
1 chilli, finely chopped (optional)
Salt and freshly ground black pepper
14 oz (397g) can peeled tomatoes

1. Par-boil the potatoes (see page 29) in salted water for 5 minutes. Drain.

2. Heat the oil in a saucepan and fry the mustard seeds until they pop (about 30 seconds).

3. Stir in the cumin, coriander and turmeric and fry gently for a few seconds.

4. Add the potatoes, onion, garlic and chilli, stirring well to coat with the spices.

5. Continue frying over a low heat for 10 minutes, stirring frequently.

6. Add the salt, pepper and tomatoes and simmer for 30-40 minutes until the potatoes are tender. Stir occasionally.

Tip: Canned whole tomatoes are considerably cheaper than the ready-chopped variety and give just as good results.

RICE

Rice makes a quick and easy accompaniment which is especially suited to dishes of a liquid consistency, e.g. curries and casseroles. Rice also forms the basis of economical risottos, pilaffs and salads, to which a wide range of ingredients is added, and recipes for these are given elsewhere in the book.

Long grain white or brown rice is used for savoury dishes. Brown rice is more chewy in texture with a pleasant nutty flavour, and is a valuable source of fibre and B vitamins. White rice is polished, a process which removes the goodness of germ and bran.

Allow 2 oz (50g) of rice per person; white rice takes about 10-15 minutes to cook and brown about 30-40 minutes. There is no need to buy exotically packaged, and expensive, rice concoctions. With a little imagination it is much cheaper to create your own interesting varieties. I use supermarket 'own brands' and by observing a few rules, good results can be achieved.

Rules For Perfect Rice

1. Excess starch prevents the rice drying out into separate grains when cooked, so it is important to wash the rice under cold running water before cooking.

2. Use the amount of water stated in the recipe; adding more makes the rice soggy.

3. Don't lift the lid or stir the rice during cooking as this releases the starch, causing the grains to clog together.

Tip: If rice is to be used cold for salads, cool it as quickly as possible. It can be kept overnight in the fridge. Rice should be re-heated quickly and must be hot right the way through before eating.

PLAIN WHITE RICE

Serves 4

Preparation time: 3 mins.   *Cooking time: 10-15 mins.*

8 oz (225g) long grain white rice
1 level teasp salt
1 pt (570ml) water

1. Wash the rice thoroughly, then put it in a saucepan with the salt and water.

2. Bring to the boil, then cover the pan and cook slowly for 10-15 minutes.

PLAIN BROWN RICE

Serves 4

Preparation time: 3 mins.   *Cooking time: 30-40 mins.*

8 oz (225g) brown rice
1 level teasp salt
1 pt (570ml) water

1. Wash the rice thoroughly, then put it in a saucepan with the salt and water.

2. Bring to the boil, then cover the pan and cook slowly for 30-40 minutes.

SIMPLE PILAU RICE

The simplest and cheapest pilau rice can be made by adding some chopped onion and a little turmeric to give a golden colour.

Preparation time: 5 mins.   *Cooking time: 5 mins.*

3 tablsp oil
1 onion, peeled and finely chopped
1 rounded teasp turmeric
8 oz (225g) cooked white or brown long grain rice

1. Heat the oil in a large frying pan and fry the onion gently for a few minutes until softened.

2. Stir in the turmeric and cook for a further few seconds.

3. Add the cooked rice and stir briskly until it is well coated with the spice and has heated through thoroughly.

VEGETABLE RICE

This recipe is just a suggestion; all sorts of bits and pieces can be added. Try a few sultanas, peanuts and drained mandarin oranges. Brown rice can be treated in the same way.

Preparation time: 5 mins.   *Cooking time: 15 mins.*

8 oz (225g) long grain white rice
1 level teasp salt
1 pt (570ml) water
4 oz (100g) frozen peas, defrosted
7 oz (198g) can sweetcorn, drained

1. Wash the rice thoroughly, then put it in a saucepan with the salt and water.

2. Bring to the boil, then cover the pan and cook slowly for 8 minutes.

3. Add the peas and sweetcorn and continue cooking for a further 6-7 minutes until the rice is tender.

SAUCES

A simple white or cheese sauce forms the basis of many of the dishes in this book, improving their flavour and appearance. Indeed, more often than not, the sauce actually makes the dish.

There is no need to buy expensive packet mixes. Making a sauce from scratch doesn't take any longer, especially if you use this one-stage method.

ONE-STAGE WHITE SAUCE

1 oz (25g) flour
1 oz (25g) margarine
½ pt (300ml) cold milk
Salt and freshly ground black pepper

1. Put the first three ingredients into a small saucepan.

2. Using a balloon or wire hand whisk, beat the liquid over a medium heat until the mixture thickens and bubbles.

3. Season to taste with salt and pepper.

CHEESE SAUCE

Make the basic white sauce, then remove from the heat and stir in 3 oz (75g) grated Cheddar cheese.

PARSLEY SAUCE   (Good with new potatoes, leeks or boiled ham.)

Make the basic white sauce, then stir in 1-2 tablespoons chopped fresh parsley and, if liked, a squeeze of lemon juice.

MUSTARD WHITE SAUCE   (Good with fish or boiled ham.)

Blend 1 level tablespoon dry mustard, 1 level teaspoon sugar and 1 tablespoon of vinegar to a smooth cream. Stir into the hot white sauce.

ONION SAUCE   (Good for boiled ham or lamb.)

Cook one small chopped onion in boiling water for 10 minutes. Drain and then stir into the basic white sauce.

GRAVY

To make standard gravy to accompany a roast joint:

Remove the meat on to a serving platter. Drain off all but the sediment and about 1 tablespoon of fat from the roasting tin. Stir in 1 tablespoon of flour and mix to a paste. Gradually pour in about ½ pint (300ml) stock or water, stirring all the time. Bring to the boil and stir for 2-3 minutes until the gravy has thickened. Season to taste with salt and freshly ground black pepper.

Tip: Don't sling goodness down the drain! Use the water in which vegetables were cooked to make the gravy.

STOCK

Home-made stock for soups is a good way of utilising ingredients which might otherwise be wasted and these include oddments of vegetables, peelings, bones, meat trimmings and chicken carcasses. Alternatively, water in which a chicken, a joint of meat or ham, or vegetables have been cooked makes instant stock.

VEGETABLE STOCK

Most vegetables can be used although I find that greens such as sprouts, cabbage and broccoli produce a too distinctive flavour. Spinach also produces a stock which is dark and dirty-looking. If a brown stock, rather than a pale colour, is preferred, add onion skins. Flavour and colour can also be enhanced by the addition of yeast extract. If you like a garlic flavour, then add garlic. Vegetable stock keeps for 3-4 days in the fridge, or stored in covered, rigid containers, it can be frozen for 2-3 months.

8 oz (225g) potatoes
2 medium sized carrots
1 onion
1 stick celery
1 tablsp oil
Sprig parsley
Sprig thyme
Bay leaf
½ level teasp salt
Few peppercorns
3 pts (1.7 litres) water

1. Scrub the vegetables thoroughly and cut them into small pieces, skins and all.

(continued overleaf)

2. Heat the oil in a saucepan and gently fry the vegetables for 8 minutes.

3. Add the herbs, salt, peppercorns and water.

4. Bring to the boil, cover and simmer gently for about 1½-2 hours. Strain before using.

MEAT OR BONE STOCK

Meat stock can be kept for a couple of days in the fridge.

Cooked or raw bones from meat or poultry
Meat trimmings (optional)
2 onions, cut into pieces
2 sticks celery, cut into pieces
2 medium sized carrots, cut into pieces
Sprig parsley and thyme
Peppercorns
½ level teasp salt
Bay leaf
3 pts (1.7 litres) water

1. Put all the ingredients into a saucepan, bring to the boil and simmer for about 3 hours.

2. Strain before use.

Simple salads are one of the nicest accompaniments to a main course and a quick way of introducing vitamins, minerals and fibre to the daily diet. What is more, making your own costs a fraction of the price you have to pay for small tubs of ready-prepared salads.

Just about any combination of salad greens, vegetables, fruit and nuts can be used imaginatively. Much of the success of a salad depends on the dressing and the simplest include mayonnaise, soured cream or oil and vinegar.

The recipes suggested here are designed to accompany more substantial meals in place of cooked vegetables. Salads, however, can be a meal in themselves and suggestions for these are given elsewhere in the book.

BASIC MIXED SALAD   *Serves 4*

½ bunch watercress
¼ iceberg lettuce, coarsely shredded
Piece cucumber, sliced or diced
2 tomatoes, sliced or quartered

Combine all the ingredients in a serving dish and pour over a little oil and vinegar dressing.

OIL AND VINEGAR DRESSING

½ pt (300ml) oil
¼ pt (150ml) vinegar
1 level teasp salt
1 level teasp sugar

(continued overleaf)

OIL AND VINEGAR DRESSING *continued*

¼ level teasp freshly ground black pepper
¼ level teasp dry mustard

Put all the ingredients in a lidded glass jar and shake vigorously until thick. The dressing can be stored for several months in the fridge but should be shaken well before each use.

Tip: To keep lettuce in good condition, cut ¼" (0.5cm) off the stalk, hold upside-down under cold running water for a few seconds, shake dry and store in the fridge.

Watercress does not stay fresh long, but it will keep for a couple of days when sealed in a polythene bag in the fridge.

NEW POTATO SALAD WITH SOURED CREAM DRESSING   *Serves 4*

Preparation time: 10 mins.   *Cooking time: 15-20 mins.*

1½ lb (700g) baby new potatoes
5 fl oz (150ml) carton soured cream
4 spring onions, chopped
½ level teasp sugar
Salt and freshly ground black pepper

1. Scrub the potatoes and cook in boiling, salted water for 15-20 minutes until tender. Drain and cool.

2. Mix the soured cream, spring onions and sugar together in a bowl.

3. Cut the potatoes in half and toss gently in the dressing. Season with salt and pepper.

WALDORF SALAD

Serves 4

Preparation time: 10 mins.   *Cooking time: None.*

3 eating apples
2 sticks celery, chopped
2 oz (50g) walnut pieces
2 tablsp mayonnaise
Freshly ground black pepper

1. Remove the peel and core from the apples and discard.
    Dice the flesh.

2. Mix the diced apple with the celery, walnuts, mayon-
    naise and pepper.

VEGETABLES

The price of more ordinary vegetables like mushrooms, carrots and onions remains fairly static throughout the year but those at the exotic end of the market such as courgettes, asparagus and even tomatoes, are cheaper at certain times. To some extent price is also governed by the weather. However, it pays to know when fruit and vegetables are in season because it can make a great difference to the household budget. The following list gives a rough guide.

Aubergines:	July-August
Beans, Broad:	June-August
, Runner:	August-October
Broccoli:	April-May, August-November
Cabbage:	All year
Carrots:	All year
Cauliflower:	June-October
Celery:	September-February
Chicory:	September-April
Courgettes:	June-September
Cress:	All year
Cucumber:	June-September
Fennel:	August-November
Leeks:	September-March
Lettuce:	May-October
Marrow:	July-October
Mushrooms:	All year
New Potatoes:	May-June
Onions:	All year
, Spring:	May-September
Parsnips:	October-March
Peas (fresh):	May-September
Peppers:	August-November
Spinach:	May-October
Sprouts:	September-March
Sweetcorn:	May-August
Tomatoes:	May, July-September

FRUIT

Fresh fruit always makes a good dessert and the following list gives a rough guide to seasons when prices reach their lowest. Make the most of the refreshing taste of raw fruit as it is packed with vitamins and needs little or no preparation or embellishment.

Apples:	All year
, home-grown:	glut in autumn
Apricots:	December-February, May-August
Bananas:	All year
Blackberries:	Autumn (pick 'free' in hedgerows)
Blackcurrants:	July
Cherries, cooking:	July-August
, eating:	June-August
Gooseberries:	June
Grapefruits:	All year
Grapes:	All year
Greengages:	July-September
Loganberries:	July-August
Melons:	June-July (cheapest)
Nectarines, home-grown:	July-August
, imported:	December-May, August-September
Oranges:	All year
Peaches, home-grown:	June-August
, imported:	January-March, June-September
Pears:	September-March
Pineapples:	June-July
Plums, home-grown:	July-September
, imported:	January-April, May-July
Raspberries:	July-August
Redcurrants:	July
Rhubarb, early or forced:	December-March
, outdoor:	March-June

Strawberries:	June-July
Tangerines, Clementines, Satsumas, Mandarins:	October-February

DRIED FRUIT

In winter months when fresh fruit is expensive, dried fruit offers an economical and nutritious alternative. Prunes, figs, apples, peaches, apricots and pears are available which are rich in fibre, protein, vitamins and minerals. Some no-soak varieties are now on the market, although other varieties will require soaking in cold water overnight before cooking.

Most dried fruit is sprayed with preservative which gives a pleasing moist appearance. Wash the fruit in hot water before cooking. Likewise sulphur dioxide is used to preserve colour; remove this by cooking the fruit in boiling water for one minute and then discard the water.

17   ENTERTAINING ON A BUDGET

Some of the dishes in this section may not be quite as quick as the recipes throughout the rest of the book, but they are all economical and straightforward. Having guests to a meal can be a nightmare if you're short of cash. Luckily for most households informal entertaining has largely replaced the more formal dinner party.

Invariably it's the hostess who presents a simple, but attractive and tasty meal who is remembered more favourably than the one who has opened exotically packaged foil cartons from a chain store and spent a fortune in the process. Psychologically a little panache goes a long way. And that's what you have to do when entertaining on a shoestring – make a few expensive ingredients stretch or make humble ingredients appear more exciting.

The standard rule in menu planning is balance. Aim for a variety of ingredients and if you serve a substantial main course, precede or follow it with something light. Finally, bear in mind that when you want to create an impression, the

presentation of food and a cheerful welcome are more important than what you spend. The following menus are designed
to cost about the same as take-away beefburgers and fries for
6 people.

SUGGESTED MENUS

Four three-course meals, one for each season, are suggested
as well as two for more informal get-togethers. The recipes
are designed to give a balance of flavours and each serves 6
people.

It's no time to experiment with guests due in an hour, so try
the ideas out beforehand to make sure you're happy with
procedures, flavours and quantities.

Spring Menu
Smoked Mackerel Pâté
    (page 98)
Pork Chasseur
    New potatoes
    Peas and carrots
Caramel Custard

Autumn Menu
Egg Mayonnaise with
    Prawns
Carbonnade of Beef
    Brown or white rice
    Baked tomatoes
Pears Belle Hélène

Informal Menus
Jambalaya
    Garlic bread
Lemon Crunch Pie

Summer Menu
Cheese Beignettes
Salmon Mousse
    Melba Toast
    Wild rice/mixed salad
Strawberry/
    Raspberry Gâteau

Winter Menu
Florida Cocktail
Steak and Mushroom Pie
    Roast potatoes and
        parsnips
    Leeks in white sauce
Profiteroles

Lasagne
    Garlic bread
    Mixed salad
Lemon Sorbet

PORK CHASSEUR

Serves 6

Supermarket freezer cabinets usually include packs of frozen pork steaks which are economical and ideal for this recipe. Serve with new potatoes, peas and carrots.

Preparation time: 10 mins.   *Cooking time: 40 mins.*

6 pork steaks
Oil
Salt and freshly ground black pepper
Knob margarine
1 large onion, peeled and chopped
6 oz (175g) mushrooms, sliced thinly
1 stock cube
14 oz (397g) can peeled tomatoes
5 fl oz (150ml) carton double cream

1.   Pre-heat oven to 180°C (350°F) or Gas No 4.

2.   Put the pork steaks in a roasting tin, brush with oil and sprinkle with salt and pepper. Roast for about 40 minutes until the pork is tender. (If using frozen meat, make sure it is thoroughly defrosted before cooking.)

3.   Meanwhile, heat 1 tablespoon of oil and the margarine in a frying pan and gently cook the onion and mushrooms for 8-10 minutes until tender.

4.   Crumble in the stock cube.

5.   Strain the tomatoes, roughly chopping them in the colander, but reserve the juice.

6.   Stir the tomato flesh into the frying pan.

7.   Now add the cream, a little salt and pepper and cook

(continued overleaf)

gently for a few minutes. If the sauce is too thick add a little of the tomato juice.

8. Transfer the pork to a serving dish and spoon over the sauce. If liked, sprinkle some chopped parsley on top.

CARAMEL CUSTARD   *Serves 6*

This popular dessert looks more attractive if cooked in individual stoneware cups or tin moulds. Alternatively, cook the custard in an ovenproof dish but it is more difficult to turn out and doesn't look so professional. For best results chill the cooked custards for several hours, or overnight, before serving.

Caramel custard is particularly nice served with a little fresh fruit and/or Continental-style biscuits.

Preparation time: 20 mins.   *Cooking time: 45 mins.*

For the caramel

5 oz (150g) caster sugar
7 fl oz (200ml) water

For the custard

1 pt (570ml) milk
1 oz (25g) caster sugar
4 size 2 eggs, beaten

1. Heat the water gently and dissolve the sugar slowly in it without boiling.

2. When thoroughly dissolved, boil until the mixture caramelises, i.e. turns light brown and syrupy.

3. Pre-heat oven to 150°C (300°F) or Gas No 2.

4. Put a thick layer of newspaper in the base of a roasting tin and half fill with water.

5. Stand 6 individual cups in the roasting tin and put in the oven to warm.

6. Bring the milk and sugar to boiling point, then pour over the beaten eggs and stir well.

7. Pour a little caramel into each warmed cup and twist it around to coat the bottom and part of the sides.

8. Strain the custard on to the caramel and cook for about 45 minutes. (One large dish will take about one hour.)

9. Remove the cups from the roasting tin and chill the custards in the fridge, preferably overnight. Loosen round the edge of the cups with a round-bladed knife and turn out into individual glass dishes.

CHEESE BEIGNETTES
Serves 6

These light cheese puffs make a tasty and economical starter. Serve 3 to 4 on a little shredded lettuce and add a garnish of sliced tomato and cucumber.

Preparation time: 20 mins.   *Cooking time: 5 mins.*

1½ oz (40g) margarine
¼ pt (150ml) water
2 oz (50g) plain flour
2 size 3 eggs, beaten
2 oz (50g) mature Cheddar cheese, grated
Salt and freshly ground black pepper
Grated Parmesan cheese for garnish (optional)
Cayenne pepper for garnish (optional)

1. Melt the margarine in the water and bring to the boil.

2. Remove from heat, add the sieved flour all at once and then beat until the mixture is smooth and leaves the sides of the pan clean.

3. Beat in the eggs little by little.

4. Stir in the grated cheese, salt and pepper.

5. Heat a deep pan of oil and fry teaspoons of the mixture for about 5 minutes until golden brown and puffy. Drain on kitchen paper.

6. Sprinkle with grated Parmesan cheese and a little cayenne pepper before serving if liked. Serve within 10 minutes of cooking.

Tip: The beignettes should sizzle gently when cooking; if the oil is too cool they will be greasy and if it is too hot they will be burnt on the outside and uncooked inside. For best results use fresh oil.

SALMON MOUSSE

Even with the lower prices in recent years of farmed fish, fresh salmon is still expensive. This light and creamy mousse is the next best thing for warm summer evenings. It can be served in any attractive dish but for a professional look use a tin mould. I use a plain ring with a hole in the middle which always turns out well.

Serve the mousse with melba toast (very thin slices of bread toasted until crisp). Commercially made versions are available. Wild rice and a good selection of salad vegetables complete the perfect accompaniments.

Preparation time: 35 mins. plus several hours chilling
Cooking time: None.

14.75 oz (418g) can red salmon
Approx. ¼ pt (150ml) milk
1 oz (25g) margarine
1½ oz (40g) flour
2 size 2 eggs, separated
1 teasp Worcestershire sauce
juice ½ lemon
Salt and freshly ground black pepper
¼ level teasp cayenne pepper (optional)
2 teasp freshly chopped dill (optional)
5 fl oz (150ml) carton double cream, lightly whipped
4 level teasp powdered gelatine
3 tablsp hot water

1. Drain the salmon and make up the liquor to ½ pt (300ml) with milk.

2. Remove any skin from the fish and flake the flesh into a bowl.

3. Put the margarine, flour, salmon liquor and milk into a small saucepan and whisk over a low heat until thickened.

(continued overleaf)

4. Remove from heat and stir in the egg yolks.

5. Stir the sauce into the salmon and leave to cool for a few minutes.

6. Stir in the Worcestershire sauce, lemon juice, salt, pepper, cayenne and dill if using and the lightly whipped cream.

7. Have ready a mould rinsed out with cold water but do not dry.

8. Sprinkle the gelatine on to the hot water and stir until dissolved. Set aside.

9. Whisk the egg whites until stiff.

10. Stir the dissolved gelatine into the salmon mixture and then fold in the egg whites thoroughly.

11. Pour the mixture into the wetted mould and chill in the fridge for several hours or overnight.

12. To turn out, dip the mould in hot water for a few seconds. Invert a wet serving plate over the top of the mould, turn over and give the mould a good hard shake to release the mousse.

13. Garnish around the edge of the mousse with thin slices of lemon and cucumber. The central hole can be filled with sprigs of watercress and/or dill.

STRAWBERRY OR RASPBERRY GÂTEAU

Serves 6

This simple and delicious dessert can be made the day before serving and is an excellent choice for a summer dinner party.

Preparation time: 40 mins.   *Cooking time: 15 mins.*

Genoese Sponge (see page 220)
1 lb (450g) strawberries OR raspberries
10 fl oz (300ml) whipping OR double cream, lightly whipped
Caster sugar

1. Make the sponge as per page 220.

2. Meanwhile, slice the strawberries, reserving a few whole ones for the top, and sprinkle with sugar. (If using raspberries, leave whole and sprinkle with sugar.)

3. When the sponge is cold, slice each horizontally and then layer back together with whipped cream, sliced strawberries or raspberries and a little of the juice.

4. Spread a layer of whipped cream over the top and decorate with whole strawberries or raspberries.

AUTUMN MENU

EGG MAYONNAISE WITH PRAWNS   *Serves 6*

Preparation time: 10 mins.   *Cooking time: 10 mins.*

6 size 3 or 4 eggs
Cress
Tomato, sliced
Cucumber, sliced
6 tablsp mayonnaise
4 oz (100g) peeled prawns
Paprika pepper (optional)

1. Hard boil the eggs for 10 minutes. Hold under cold running water to prevent discolouration.

2. Meanwhile, arrange a little cress and a slice or two of tomato and cucumber on six small plates.

3. Shell and cut the eggs in two and place cut side down on the cress.

4. Spoon a little mayonnaise over the eggs and top with prawns.

5. Sprinkle with paprika if liked.

CARBONNADE OF BEEF   *Serves 6*

Beef cooked in beer is a classic tasty casserole. It is almost impossible to spoil so is ideal if unreliable guests are expected!

Preparation time: 10 mins.   *Cooking time: 2 hours*

2 lb (900g) chuck steak, cubed
1 large onion, peeled and roughly chopped

2 cloves garlic, peeled and finely chopped
2 tablsp oil
2 tablsp flour
2 teasp mustard powder
2 teasp soft brown sugar
2 teasp vinegar
Salt and freshly ground black pepper
1 level teasp mixed dried herbs OR 1 tablsp chopped
   fresh herbs
1 beef stock cube
½ pt (300ml) water
½ pt (300ml) beer or brown ale

1. Fry the meat, onion and garlic in the oil for about 10 minutes.

2. Meanwhile, pre-heat oven to 150°C (300°F) or Gas No 2.

3. Stir the flour, mustard powder, brown sugar, vinegar, salt, pepper, herbs and crumbled stock cube into the meat and onion.

4. Transfer the mixture to a lidded ovenproof casserole and stir in the water and beer or brown ale. Mix well.

5. Cook for about 2 hours until the meat is tender, stirring occasionally.

Tip: The carbonnade can be served with plain boiled or pilau rice and green vegetables. However, for the authentic French way, use a bread and mustard topping. Simply cut out 6 rounds from thin slices of bread, spread them with French mustard and pop the rounds on top of the carbonnade 15 minutes before serving. Return to the oven without a lid to crisp the bread.

PEARS BELLE HÉLÈNE

This is a classic dessert of pears and ice cream topped with chocolate sauce. Use ripe plump pears and good quality ice cream.

Preparation time: 20 mins.   *Cooking time: None.*

4 oz (100g) plain chocolate
1 oz (25g) butter or margarine
2 tablsp milk
3 juicy pears
6 scoops vanilla ice cream

1. Put the chocolate and butter or margarine in a bowl and stand it in a saucepan of hot water to melt.

2. When well blended, stir in the milk.

3. Meanwhile, cut each pear in half and remove the skin and core.

4. Put a scoop of ice cream in 6 individual glass bowls, top with a pear half and pour over a little chocolate sauce.

FLORIDA COCKTAIL

Serves 6

This makes a light refreshing starter to the two hearty courses which follow.

Preparation time: 20 mins.   *Cooking time: None.*

3 grapefruit
3 oranges
6 glacé OR marachino cherries (optional)
Caster sugar

1. Segment the grapefruit and oranges as follows: using a small sharp knife, remove the skin and pith by following the contour of the fruit. The flesh should be exposed. Holding the fruit in one hand over a basin, remove the segments by cutting down each side of the membrane. Finally, squeeze the pulp to extract the juice.

2. Arrange the fruit attractively in six shallow glass bowls and top with a cherry.

3. Sprinkle a little caster sugar over the top.

STEAK AND MUSHROOM PIE

Serves 6

Few people can resist a home-made pie with tender chunks of meat and mushroom, cooked in a dark rich gravy and topped with a thick crust.

Preparation time: 15 mins.   *Cooking time: 2 hours.*

1½ lb (700g) chuck steak, cubed
1 large onion, peeled and roughly chopped
2 tablsp oil
8 oz (225g) large mushrooms, cut into pieces

(continued overleaf)

1 tablsp flour
1 beef stock cube
Salt and freshly ground black pepper
½ pt (300ml) water
8 oz (225g) short crust pastry (see page 234 or use frozen,
   defrosted)

1. Pre-heat oven to 150°C (300°F) or Gas No 2.

2. Fry the meat and onion in the oil for about 5 minutes.

3. Stir in the mushrooms and cook for a further 5 minutes.

4. Turn the meat and vegetables into a lidded casserole and stir in the flour, crumbled stock cube, salt, pepper and water.

5. Cook for about 1½ hours until the meat is tender, stirring occasionally.

6. Meanwhile, make the pastry as per page 234, unless using frozen, defrosted.

7. Turn the cooked meat mixture into an ovenproof pie dish and allow to cool slightly.

8. Meanwhile, turn the oven up to 200°C (400°F) or Gas No 6.

9. Roll out the pastry slightly larger than the top of the pie dish. Next, cut off a strip from around the edge of the pastry, dampen the edge of the pie dish, and put the strip on it.

10. Dampen the strip and then use the remaining pastry to cover the pie. Trim off excess pastry and pinch the edges between thumb and forefinger.

11. Make a cross in the top of the pie with a sharp knife, cutting right through the pastry to allow the steam to escape, then brush the pastry with beaten egg or milk.

12. Bake for 20 minutes until nicely browned.

PROFITEROLES

Compared to buying ready-made these are cheap to make, if not a bit fiddly, but delicious!

Preparation time: 40 mins.   *Cooking time: 15-20 mins.*

1 oz (25g) margarine
¼ pt (150ml) water
2½ oz (75g) plain flour, sieved
2 size 4 eggs, beaten
5 fl oz (150ml) carton whipping OR double cream
2 oz (50g) plain chocolate
6 oz (175g) icing sugar

1. Pre-heat oven to 200°C (400°F) or Gas No 6.

2. Melt the margarine in the water and bring to the boil.

3. Remove from heat, add the flour all at once and beat until the mixture forms a ball and leaves the side of the pan clean.

4. Gradually beat in the beaten eggs, beating well between each addition. (An electric beater makes the job less tiring.)

5. Put teaspoons of the mixture on to a wetted baking tray, spacing well apart, and bake for 15 to 20 minutes until crisp and golden brown. Cool on a wire rack.

6. Whip the cream until it just holds its shape.

7. Make a small hole in the bottom of each profiterole and spoon in a little cream. (The job is made much easier with a piping bag; if you don't have one see 'tip' below for making paper version.)

8. Now make the chocolate topping: put the chocolate in a cup and stand it in a pan of hot water to melt. Do not overheat. Stir in a tablespoon of hot water and mix well.

(continued overleaf)

9. Sieve the icing sugar into a bowl and stir in the chocolate. Add a little cold water if necessary to make a thick coating consistency.

10. Pile the profiteroles in a glass bowl and trickle over the chocolate topping.

Tip: To make a paper icing bag, fold a 10" (25cm) square of greaseproof or non-stick paper diagonally into a triangle. Holding the right angle of the triangle towards you, roll over one of the corners to meet it. Roll the second corner over in the opposite direction to meet the first at the back of the bag, thus forming a cone shape. Fold over the edges several times to secure the bag in place. Cut a small piece off the tip of the bag. Put in a little whipped cream and fold the top over.

INFORMAL MENUS

JAMBALAYA   *Serves 6*

This hot and gutsy dish from the southern states of America is a good choice for informal entertaining. Add as many chillies as you dare but one is probably enough for the average person! Serve with plenty of garlic bread.

Preparation time: 20 mins.   *Cooking time: 30 mins.*

2 tablsp oil
1 large onion, peeled and chopped
1 or more chillies (depending on taste), finely chopped
1 green pepper, sliced
2 sticks celery, sliced

2 cloves garlic, peeled and finely chopped
8 oz (225g) belly or pork strips, cut into small pieces
10 oz (285g) long grain rice
1 tablsp freshly chopped marjoram OR basil
14 oz (397g) can peeled tomatoes
6 oz (170g) smoked sausage, sliced
4 oz (100g) ham, sliced into strips
2 rounded teasp soft brown OR demerara sugar
Salt and freshly ground black pepper
1½ pts (700ml) water
4 oz (100g) peeled prawns
3 spring onions, sliced

1. Heat the oil and fry the onion, chilli, green pepper, celery, garlic and pork for 10 minutes.

2. Add the rice and stir for a couple of minutes until translucent.

3. Stir in the herbs, tomatoes, sausage, ham, sugar, salt, pepper and water.

4. Bring to the boil, put a lid on the pan and simmer very gently for about 30 minutes until most of the liquid has been absorbed and the rice is tender.

5. Stir in the prawns and spring onions and cook for a further minute.

6. Turn into a large serving bowl.

Tip: Make up your own version of this recipe substituting various ingredients with whatever you can find at the right price. Strips of chicken, for example, could be used instead of pork, or a couple of courgettes in place of the green pepper.

LEMON CRUNCH PIE

A tangy creamy filling in a crunchy biscuit case. A great favourite! The dish improves if made the day before eating.

Preparation time: 30 mins.   *Cooking time: None.*

4 oz (100g) margarine
7 oz (200g) packet ginger nut biscuits
7 oz (200g) can condensed milk
Juice and finely grated rind of 2 large lemons
5 fl oz (150ml) carton double cream
1 small lemon for decoration

1. Melt the margarine in a medium sized saucepan.

2. Meanwhile, crush the biscuits by putting them in a small polythene bag and bashing with a rolling pin.

3. Tip the crushed biscuits into the margarine and mix very well.

4. Using the back of a wooden spoon press the mixture into a shallow 8" (20.5cm) pie dish, making a case for the filling.

5. Put the condensed milk in a bowl and gradually whisk in the lemon juice and grated rind.

6. Whip the cream until it just holds its shape, but not too stiff, then fold it into the lemon mixture. (If liked a little can be reserved for piping some stars on the top.)

7. Pour the mixture into the biscuit case and chill for several hours before serving.

8. Decorate with thin slices of lemon.

LASAGNE

This is a popular choice for informal entertaining. Serve with garlic bread and a mixed salad of lettuce, watercress, cucumber, spring onions and tomato. Use lasagne marked 'no pre-cooking required'.

Preparation time: 15 mins.   *Cooking time: 40 mins.*

1½ tablsp oil
1 large onion, peeled and chopped
6 oz (175g) button mushrooms, sliced
1 lb (450g) minced beef
1 tablsp flour
1 tablsp tomato purée
Salt and freshly ground black pepper
1 tablsp freshly chopped basil
14 oz (397g) can peeled tomatoes
¼ pt (150ml) water
Approx. 6 or 7 sheets lasagne
½ pt (300ml) cheese sauce (see page 249) or use 1 packet
   (17g size) white sauce mix and add 3 oz grated
   Cheddar cheese
1 oz (25g) Cheddar cheese, grated (for topping)

1. Heat the oil and sauté the onion and mushrooms for 10 minutes.

2. Add the beef, breaking it down with a fork, and fry until brown, about 5 minutes.

3. Stir in the flour, tomato purée, salt, pepper, basil, tomatoes and water.

4. Mix well while bringing to the boil, then simmer for a couple of minutes.

5. Alternate layers of lasagne and meat mixture in a shallow ovenproof dish, ending with lasagne.

(continued overleaf)

6. Pre-heat oven to 180°C (350°F) or Gas No 4.

7. Make the cheese sauce as per page 249 (or make up the white sauce mix following manufacturer's instructions, adding 3 oz grated Cheddar). Pour over the lasagne.

8. Sprinkle the grated cheese on top.

9. Bake for about 20 minutes until the cheese is brown and bubbly.

LEMON SORBET   *Serves 6*

Sorbets can be made so much more cheaply than buying and the lemon variety is one of the easiest. Serve with Continental-style wafers or delicate biscuits.

Preparation time: 10 mins. plus 12 hours freezing time
Cooking time: 10 mins.

8 oz (225g) caster sugar
1 pt (570ml) water
Thinly pared rind and juice of 3 lemons
2 egg whites

1. Dissolve the sugar in the water over a low heat.

2. Add the lemon rind and boil gently for 10 minutes.

3. Stir in the lemon juice and leave to cool.

4. Strain the liquid into a freezing tray or shallow dish and freeze until mushy.

5. Whisk the egg whites until stiff and then mix thoroughly into the lemon mixture.

6. Pour into a plastic lidded container and freeze for at least 12 hours before serving.

Tip: Use up the egg yolks in a quiche, bacon and egg pie, or omelette, or mix with a little milk and use to glaze pastry before cooking.

GENERAL INDEX

INDEX OF RECIPES

287